AQA Media Studies for A-level
CLOSE STUDY PRODUCTS

Stephanie Hendry
Elspeth Stevenson
Diane Naylor

Approval message from AQA
This textbook has been approved by AQA for use with our qualification. This means that we have checked that it broadly covers the specification and we are satisfied with the overall quality. Full details of our approval process can be found on our website.

We approve textbooks because we know how important it is for teachers and students to have the right resources to support their teaching and learning. However, the publisher is ultimately responsible for the editorial control and quality of this book.

Please note that when teaching the **AQA Media Studies for A-level** course, you must refer to AQA's specification as your definitive source of information. While this book has been written to match the specification, it cannot provide complete coverage of every aspect of the course.

A wide range of other useful resources can be found on the relevant subject pages of our website: **www.aqa.org.uk**.

Although every effort has been made to ensure that website addresses are correct at time of going to press, Hodder Education cannot be held responsible for the content of any website mentioned in this book. It is sometimes possible to find a relocated web page by typing in the address of the home page for a website in the URL window of your browser.

Hachette UK's policy is to use papers that are natural, renewable and recyclable products and made from wood grown in well-managed forests and other controlled sources. The logging and manufacturing processes are expected to conform to the environmental regulations of the country of origin.

To order, please visit www.hoddereducation.com or contact Customer Service at education@hachette.co.uk / +44 (0)1235 827827.

ISBN: 978 1 3983 8802 4

© Stephanie Hendry, Elspeth Stevenson and Diane Naylor 2024

First published in 2024 by Hodder Education.

An Hachette UK Company
Carmelite House
50 Victoria Embankment
London EC4Y 0DZ

www.hoddereducation.com

Impression number   10 9 8 7 6 5 4 3 2 1

Year   2028 2027 2026 2025 2024

All rights reserved. Apart from any use permitted under UK copyright law, no part of this publication may be reproduced or transmitted in any form or by any means, electronic or mechanical, including photocopying and recording, or held within any information storage and retrieval system, without permission in writing from the publisher or under licence from the Copyright Licensing Agency Limited. Further details of such licences (for reprographic reproduction) may be obtained from the Copyright Licensing Agency Limited, www.cla.co.uk

Cover photo © Pawel Horazy – stock.adobe.com

Illustrations by Integra Software Services

Typeset in India by Integra Software Services

Produced by DZS Grafik, Printed in Slovenia

A catalogue record for this title is available from the British Library.

CONTENTS

	Introduction	iv
CSP 1	'Old Town Road' – Lil Nas X with Billy Ray Cyrus	2
CSP 2	Sephora – 'Black Beauty is Beauty'	8
CSP 3	The Guardian	16
CSP 4	Blinded by the Light	24
CSP 5	Newsbeat	29
CSP 6	Zendaya's social media	37
CSP 7	The Killing	47
CSP 8	Lupin	61
CSP 9	GQ	71
CSP 10	Horizon Forbidden West	80

Introduction

The two A-level Media Studies examinations ask you to show your knowledge and understanding of the theoretical framework. To do this, you will need to offer examples from the close study media products (CSPs) set by the exam board. The CSPs are taken from nine media forms and are divided into two types:

- **Targeted CSPs**, which should be approached using selected areas from the framework (assessed in Paper 1).
- **In-depth CSPs**, which you should study using all aspects of the theoretical framework (assessed in Paper 2).

Chapter 11 of the A Level Media Studies Student Book provides advice and guidance on each of the Media Studies exam papers.

You currently need to study a total of 17 CSPs. This book provides analysis of 10 of them – at least one from each media form. The CSP case studies here should be used in conjunction with the Student Book, which focuses on the theoretical concepts you need to learn and apply.

This book demonstrates the application of these ideas and provides suggested approaches to the following media products:

Media One

Chapter	Media form	Close study product	Theoretical focus	To be studied with*
1	Music video	'Old Town Road'	Media language and representations	'Ghost Town'
2	Advertising and marketing	Sephora 'Black Beauty is Beauty'	Media language and representations	Score advert
3	Newspaper	The Guardian	Audience and industry	The Daily Mail
4	Film	Blinded by the Light	Industry	n/a
5	Radio	Newsbeat	Audience and industry	The War of the Worlds

Media Two

Chapter	Media form	Close study product	Theoretical focus	To be studied with*
6	Online, social and participatory media	Zendaya's social media**	All areas of the framework	The Voice online
7	Television	The Killing	All areas of the framework	No Offence
8	Television	Lupin	All areas of the framework	The Responder
9	Magazines	GQ	All areas of the framework	The Gentlewoman
10	Video games	Horizon Forbidden West	All areas of the framework	SIMS FreePlay

* The CSPs listed here are correct at the time of publication, but you should check the CSP booklet published each year by AQA to see if any changes have been made for your examination.

** Please note: 2024 is the final assessment year for the Zendaya social media CSP. From 2025 it will be replaced with Taylor Swift's social media.

Each chapter of this book discusses one product and demonstrates, using examples and analysis, how ideas from the appropriate areas of the theoretical framework can be applied. The case studies demonstrate the practical application of ideas from the theoretical framework.

Depending on the focus of study required for the exam, these case studies:

- use media terminology to examine the use of media language in the construction of media products and the way this creates meaning
- engage with representations and reflect on the ideas and values communicated by the product
- consider the importance of the target audience and discuss ideas related to audience behaviours and the effects of the media
- provide information about the industrial context and consider its significance
- discuss relevant contextual issues related to each CSP.

These case studies should not, however, be seen as definitive ways to think about these products, as your own engagement with the theoretical framework and with the products will allow you to make your own interpretations using your own examples. These case studies should be seen as *examples* and will provide you with support in developing your own studies on these products.

Each chapter offers the following features:

- **Links** to relevant chapters of the Student Book or useful websites.
- **Apply it** – prompts to encourage you to work with the ideas being discussed for yourself.
- **Quick questions** to help you extend your application of the ideas being discussed. (Suggested answers to quick questions are available at: www.hoddereducation.com/AQAMediaCSP.)

CSP 1: 'Old Town Road' – Lil Nas X with Billy Ray Cyrus

- **Platform**: broadcast
- **Form**: music video
- **Product**: 'Old Town Road' official movie directed by Calmatic (Charles Kidd II)
- **Targeted elements of the theoretical framework**: media language and representations
- **Assessment information**: 'Old Town Road' may appear in Paper 1, Section A. You also need to study 'Ghost Town' by The Specials, and may be asked to compare 'Old Town Road' with an unseen product.

We will consider some of the theories from the theoretical area of media language (including genre and narrative) as well as some relevant contextual knowledge.

Economic and cultural context

'Old Town Road' is the debut single by American rapper Lil Nas X (real name Montero Lamar Hill), first released independently in December 2018 on SoundCloud. The single was re-released on 5 April 2019 by Columbia Records, featuring a remix with country singer Billy Ray Cyrus. Both versions were included on Lil Nas X's second EP, entitled *7* (2019). The music video was directed by Calmatic and features cameo appearances from comedians Chris Rock and HaHa Davis, rappers Vince Staples and Rico Nasty, songwriter Jozzy, producer YoungKio and DJ Diplo. The song had sold 10 million copies in the US by October 2019, the fastest to reach this milestone. The remix featuring Billy Ray Cyrus was nominated for Record of the Year and won Best Pop Duo/Group Performance and Best Music Video at the 2020 Grammy Awards.

▲ Lil Nas X and Billy Ray Cyrus

'Old Town Road' is an example of how the music industry has adapted to a digital era of music production and promotion. Before the internet, record companies (labels) operated with a top-down (structured hierarchical) approach and they were the gatekeepers (controllers) to an artist's success. They would hire A & R (artist and repertoire) representatives to scout for new talent at shows, listen to demo tapes and monitor whether the artists were gaining in popularity; they would then sign them directly and develop their talent. Nowadays, A & R people tend to use social media to find out which artists have the largest following and who can make the most money for the record label.

▲ Calmatic

Lil Nas X is an example of this approach. He had a very quick rise to stardom. His self-produced track 'Old Town Road' reached 15 on the *Billboard* Hot 100 and number 1 on its country chart, although *Billboard* later said the track was not 'country enough' and removed it. This caused controversy around how music genres are defined and gave the track and Lil Nas X extra publicity. This was prior to his deal with major record label Columbia.

Furthermore, radio stations eager to capitalise on the track's social media popularity played the track from YouTube because it was not available through the traditional channels.

The track was not fully original, in that it sampled YoungKio's (a Dutch record producer) 'Future-type/Kodak Black-type Beat', which in turn sampled from Nine Inch Nails' *Ghosts* album. Lil Nas X bought the beat for just $30 and used it as a backing track. Strictly speaking the beat should never have been used for commercial purposes and Columbia could have run into copyright issues, but Trent Reznor from Nine Inch Nails happily approved the sample and he is now listed as a producer and songwriter on the track. The track's original video was a montage of images from the video game *Red Dead Redemption 2*. This was an initially self-produced media product that had a grassroots feel to it ('authentic' and personal, without the typical record company input) and quickly went viral.

In December 2018, Lil Nas X used Twitter (now X) to persuade Billy Ray Cyrus to join him on his version of 'Old Town Road'. Later, Cyrus responded to Lil Nas being taken out of the country charts by remixing the track to feature him singing on it.

It took Lil Nas X just 16 months to become a global phenomenon with 'Old Town Road', and his knowledge of social media was a major factor in how this happened. First, he was a fan of Nicki Minaj and ran an anonymous Twitter account named @nasmaraj. Minaj is known for having a huge fan base of Stans (over-zealous fans on social media) nicknamed Barbz. Lil Nas only later admitted running the account, citing being outed as a gay rapper to explain why he originally denied ownership. By dealing in memes, viral threads, engagement bait and Nicki Minaj stanning, he was able to create a six-digit follower base on Twitter, a process known as tweetdecking (using a free Twitter tool that allows users to monitor multiple timelines on a single screen). Lil Nas was able to manipulate the algorithm to get his account seen more and this served as a springboard to release 'Old Town Road'.

Lil Nas X also listed the song on iTunes and SoundCloud as country not rap, referring to the track as 'Country-Trap' to exploit the space between the two genres, a concept known as genre-straddling. This manipulated the algorithm in favour of the track where it could avoid direct competition with the more popular genres, specifically rap, which is an already saturated market. By asking users on Reddit what he should call the song, Lil Nas also utilised SEO (search-engine optimisation), which kept his content visible and at the top of the algorithm search pattern, creating more views.

There was also a certain amount of luck involved in 'Old Town Road' going viral. The release of the original track coincided with a resurgence of interest in cowboy culture, known as the #Yeehaw Agenda. The proliferation of cowboy-style memes and the release of the western-themed game *Red Dead Redemption 2* meant that audiences were already primed for content like this. The track really gained traction when it was shared on TikTok as the 'Yeehaw Challenge'. Lil Nas X even attributes much of his success to the platform. After visiting TikTok's offices in Los Angeles, he stated that TikTok helped him change his life and brought his song to several different audiences at once (newsroom.tiktok.com/en-us/lil-nas-x-takes-the-old-town-road-from-tiktok-to-the-top-of-the-charts).

> **Quick question**
> Discuss possible reasons why *Billboard*'s exclusion of 'Old Town Road' from the country charts caused controversy.

> **Apply it**
> Listen to the panel discussion 'Are Streamers the Future Labels?' from Midem 2019, youtube.com/watch?v=ObvPMWa9mQc.
>
> Sponsored by rights management organisation Sound Exchange, this event discusses how streaming sites such as Apple and Amuse may be challenging the traditional music companies and how they have the capabilities to offer musicians advances and marketing budgets for their work, especially since terrestrial radio is playing less of a part in marketing music artists.
>
> What are the potential advantages and disadvantages for music artists who decide to use these platforms?

> **Apply it**
> Look through Lil Nas X's social media posts on Twitter, Instagram and Tik Tok before and after 'Old Town Road'. How have his interactions with his audience changed? What might this reveal about the impact of being a signed artist instead of self-produced?

> **Quick question**
> What were the reasons for 'Old Town Road' going viral?

Economic and cultural context

△ Poster for Sergio Leone's *Once Upon a Time in the West* (1968)

Apply it

Watch 'Old Town Road' and identify when it uses western genre codes and conventions.

What are your initial thoughts on how the video is using them?

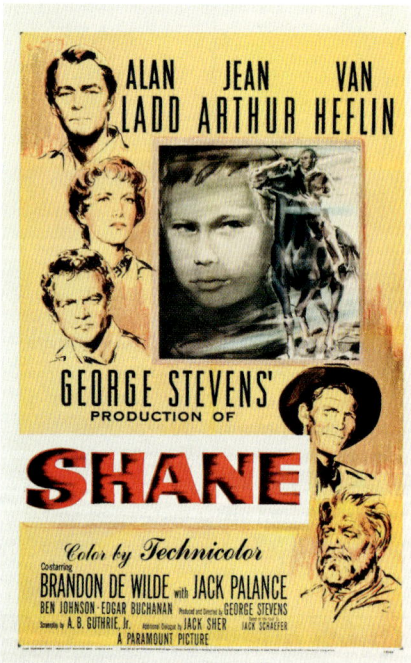

△ *Shane* (1953, directed by George Stevens) was an **archetypal** western narrative: the lone mysterious rider settles into town, escaping some unknown previous life, only to be called forth once more to save the town from conflict

Media language, narrative and genre

'Old Town Road' utilises the codes and conventions of western novels and films and reimagines them in music video form. These conventions have evolved over time and have become deeply ingrained in the genre, shaping the way the stories are told and perceived by audiences. Some conventions of westerns are:

- **Settings** – The American Old West of the 1800s, which includes vast prairies and mountains, often depicting the frontier land as an isolated and harsh wilderness to be explored, traversed or colonised.
- **Characters** – The main protagonist is typically a stoic gunslinger or cowboy who has strong moral values but is haunted by a troubled past. The antagonist is often portrayed as a ruthless outlaw or corrupt authority figure who challenges the hero's principles. Other common character types include the wise old mentor, the femme fatale, the damsel in distress, the negative stereotype of the 'savage' indigenous American and various sidekicks or companions.
- **Conflicts** – These can be external or internal. External conflicts involve struggles for power between lawmen and outlaws, settlers and native Americans, or rival factions fighting for control over land and resources. Internal conflicts focus on the personal struggles faced by the characters.
- **Visual style** – Westerns have developed a distinct visual style, with sweeping landscapes often coloured with earthy tones and epic long shots to emphasise rugged mountains and dramatic sunsets. Iconic imagery is used, such as cowboy hats, horses, tumbleweed and saloons.

■ Codes and conventions and intertextuality

The western tends to incorporate mythical elements that elevate the genre beyond a mere fictional representation of the past, often including the epic pursuit for personal identity, revenge or redemption. Furthermore, various elements within westerns have taken on symbolic meaning, for example horses as freedom, guns power and violence and the frontier as a place of adventure and individual possibility. Set in 1899, the 'Old Town Road' video is a quest narrative. Lil Nas X must escape the confines of the past to achieve fame and success, which he does with the supernatural aid of a magical horse that can accelerate at great speed and the appearance of an improbable deus ex machina (a person or thing that appears or is introduced into a situation suddenly and unexpectedly and provides an artificial or contrived solution to a problem), in the form of a wormhole to the new frontier land of Los Angeles. The earlier shots are coloured using sepia tone and echo the earthy feel of many westerns, which could create a more nostalgic view of America and would be familiar to audiences.

Established groups in westerns, such as families and small towns, were generally suspicious of outsiders. The video intertextualises this in the homestead scene, in which the father, protecting his daughter, takes aim at the duo. This is juxtaposed with the modern-day awe-struck reaction of the young boy who calls for his '*momma*' after Lil Nas drops out of nowhere, signalling the change in attitudes towards strangers.

The slow tracking shot through the mise en scène of the suburban streets captures the incredulous faces: one person takes a photo of Lil Nas, another peeps from behind a door, some appear impassive, but all of them look and gaze at the anachronistic stranger riding into town. Typically in a western, the outsider would face some conflict, or a series of trials and complications (Todorov), but in 'Old Town Road', these are replaced with harmless interactions, for example comical dance-offs rather than gunslinger stand-offs, a car versus horse race in place of a shoot-out or wagon chase, a trip to the shopping mall and impromptu performance in a village hall instead of a trip to the saloon and its cabaret.

A montage of images reinforces the conspicuous consumption of material goods. The Maserati car, the dollar sign, diamonds, rhinestones, the Super Mall, flashy suits and high-end sunglasses connote the capitalist nature of the US. Furthermore, material riches can be seen as a mytheme – Vladimir Propp noted that the hero would often be given riches and wealth as a reward for his labours (he called this transfiguration). The signifiers of wealth, such as clutching a money bag with a dollar sign on it, construct the hyperreality of the American Dream, a cultural myth that claims everyone can pursue opportunities, especially when it comes to success and wealth.

The resolution of the video has shots of Lil Nas X hugging a little bingo-playing, line-dancing, old white lady, subverting a negative stereotype of the threatening black man as well as suggesting that there is no need to fear outsiders. This culminates in a message that constructs themes of inclusivity and community above fear and violence. The humour and parody of the western is anchored by the close-up shot of Chris Rock saying 'boogity-boogity', a cultural reference that means 'quickly' and ends the video on a positive preferred reading for Lil Nas X as an inspiring individual.

■ Thomas Schatz – genres of order and integration

Thomas Schatz argued that there are two genres: the genre of order and the genre of integration.

▽ Characteristics of genres of order and genres of integration

Order e.g. western, gangster, detective	Integration e.g. musical, screwball comedy, family melodrama
Individual (male dominant)	Couple/collective (female dominant)
Contested space (ideologically unstable)	Civilised space (ideologically stable)
Externalised – violent	Internalised – emotional
Extermination – death	Embrace – love
Mediation – redemption	Integration – domestication
Macho code	Maternal/familial code
Isolated self-reliance	Community cooperation
Utopia as a promise	Utopia as reality

Traditionally, westerns follow conventions of the genre of order, but 'Old Town Road' subverts these conventions. Instead of a dominant male is the duo of Lil Nas X and Billy Ray Cyrus, who are more reminiscent of the genre of integration. There is little contested ideological space either: both the past and the present in the video foreground the idea of capitalism and there are many signs in the video that give a positive preferred reading to having wealth – dollar signs, luxury brands, jewels and references to sports cars. There is no violence; any conflict is easily resolved – for example after the car and horse race, the loser (played by Vince Staples) just 'flocks on up' (hands over) the winnings. The next shot sees Lil Nas using the money for consumer goods. This could suggest that Los Angeles, and the US as a whole, is a place that offers the 'utopia as promise' element of the genre of

△ *Butch Cassidy and the Sundance Kid* (1969, directed by George Roy Hill) featured a duo of loveable-rogue outlaws similar to Lil Nas X and Billy Ray Cyrus

Apply it
Choose three more examples from the video and analyse the connotations closely. Explore what they say about:
■ Lil Nas X as a new artist
■ America.

Media language, narrative and genre

order. Neither Lil Nas X nor Billy Ray Cyrus behaves in a particularly macho way – they do not fight the man and his daughter and they embrace love and community and cooperation, even if they are viewed with suspicion at first. These conventions seem to be a closer fit to the genre of integration.

Representations

■ Masculinity and the cowboy

Music companies need to represent their new stars effectively in music videos to establish their personas to an audience. Given the song's lyrics and previous incarnations linked to cowboy iconography, the video capitalises on these ideas to introduce Lil Nas X to a mainstream audience.

The cowboy is an instantly recognisable, romanticised figure and has featured on radio, in comic books, games, films and television shows, has had music written about him and been featured in advertising. In the past, westerns featured Wasp (white Anglo Saxon protestant) protagonists who were often misfits but who also upheld a distinctly white Christian version of American masculinity. There were mainly two types of cowboy: the strong, silent, man-of-action, often played by actors like Gary Cooper and John Wayne; and the Buffalo Bill type, who was mostly depicted showing off tricks with a particular horse – the actor Tom Mix was the prototype for this version.

Furthermore, before 1964, in a segregated USA, westerns were made only for white audiences, and any films starring black actors – called 'race films' – were shown only to black audiences. White audiences, therefore, only saw films that glorified the oppression of people of colour, who were either represented as foils for the hero or as barbaric or noble 'savages'. The idealised masculine figures that John Wayne portrayed are now seen as embodying a no holds-barred approach of policing and 'civilising' people of colour. This whitewashed the real history of cowboys, as many were in fact of Mexican and black ethnicities.

△ Tom Mix and his speedy horse in *The Speed Maniac* (1919, directed by Edward LeSaint). This cowboy figure is referenced in the 'Old Town Road' video with Lil Nas X going at impossible speeds on his horse

△ John Wayne in *The Searchers* (1956, directed by John Ford)

The Marlboro Man is another stereotypical example of the cowboy representation in American culture. Harnessed by tobacco advertising campaigns for Marlboro cigarettes, it was first conceived by Leo Burnett and used from 1954 to 1999. Presented in picturesque wild terrain, the cowboy was a rugged, free-spirited individual. The advertisements were originally conceived as a way to popularise a particular brand of filtered cigarettes – which at the time was considered feminine – by hyper-masculinising the product so it appealed to a different target audience. 'Old Town Road' intertextualises this representation when Billy Ray Cyrus references the Marlboro Man in the lyrics. Today, tobacco advertising is banned.

The music video subverts the traditional gender coding of the cowboy by juxtaposing two versions of Lil Nas: the stereotypical confident, slightly macho outsider, constructed through the leather chaps and brown cowboy hat, and the boyish, camp, country music version complete with rhinestones, jewellery and a bright smile. Billy Ray Cyrus is encoded in stereotypical feminine colours with the pink suit and flowers, highlighting Judith Butler's argument that 'the inner truth (of gender) is a fabrication' and that masculine representations can change and evolve. Both performers have been dressed extravagantly with a highly stylised camp aesthetic that is flamboyant and decorative.

Furthermore, Lil Nas X is an out gay man, adding further expansion of meaning to the traditional cowboy representation. The representation of Lil Nas in the video grafts new meaning onto the cowboy representation to subtly introduce Lil Nas as a gay country rap star, a version that has not been seen in the mainstream.

▲ The Marlboro Man

Quick question

Why do you think Columbia supported Lil Nas X duetting with Billy Ray Cyrus rather than performing alone?

Apply it

- Watch the music video for 'MONTERO (Call Me By Your Name)' by Lil Nas X (youtube.com/watch?v=6swmTBVI83k). In what ways does it construct different versions of masculinity and of Lil Nas X from those in 'Old Town Road'?
- Compare 'Old Town Road' with two other versions of black masculinity in music. How do they differ? Discuss why.

▲ Lil Nas X with Diplo, both wearing cowboy hats

Representations

CSP 2 Sephora – 'Black Beauty is Beauty'

- **Platform:** web and television
- **Form:** audiovisual media: advertising and marketing
- **Product:** advertisement
- **Targeted elements of the theoretical framework:** media language and representations, social and cultural context
- **Assessment information:** The Sephora advert is studied alongside another CSP, a historical advert for men's hair cream, Score. The products appear in Section A of Paper 1. You could be asked a short question on this advert or Score alone, or asked to compare them in a longer, 20-mark question.

This CSP is a one-minute advert that first appeared in 2021. It was made for French beauty brand Sephora, which has a successful global beauty retail business operating in 34 countries worldwide as well as online. This advert was broadcast online and on US television channels aimed specifically at black audiences.

▲ A Sephora store front in New York

Media language

■ Mise en scène and semiotics

The advertisement can be found at youtube.com/watch?v=0iOdVGzNVaI. You can use this to find the following shots of mise en scène analysis.

In the opening shot of the advert at 0:01, we see a salon for black hair.

- The pictures on the walls of the salon celebrate black beauty and emphasise the significance of hair styling to beauty culture in general, and the distinctive qualities of styling for black hair.

- The advert uses ordinary women with casual dress codes, strongly signifying that black beauty is for everyone.
- Connections with fashion and beauty culture and a relaxed atmosphere are connoted by the busy decor and the presence of magazines, reinforcing the important role of beauty culture in women's lives.

At 0:07, a split screen depicts a modern make-up palette and a historical photograph of a hair salon.

- The split screen connects the product directly with history – the branded make-up palette is explicitly connected with historical beauty practices in placing them side by side.
- Use of archive footage lends a feeling of nostalgia and authenticity to the brand message.
- A close-up of the product makes it look bright, rich and appealing.

At 0:25, we see a mother styling her young daughter's hair.

- Warm lighting and colour codes with homely decor and family photographs connote positive messages about beauty.
- The central positioning of the mother and daughter highlight close family bonds reinforced by beauty practices, and centres an ordinary woman and child in a domestic setting, elevating their importance.
- Non-verbal codes signify harmonious family relationships.

At 0:29, we see a young man and two women in one of their homes preparing their skin in carnival costumes.

- Elaborate dress code signifies carnival preparations (an arbitrary sign).
- The range of skin tones and genders are selected to connote diversity and inclusiveness.
- Juxtaposition of the home setting with costumes gives a sense of excitement – dressing up for a special event.

At 0:34, we see a woman in her kitchen making her own skincare preparations.

- The dress code is flamboyant with bright colours and statement jewellery and signifies fun as well as heritage and tradition in fashion.
- Care and attention to process is signified by careful selection of homemade ingredients for a product, showing knowledge.
- Again, a domestic location is used to position the brand at the heart of home life as well as community events.

Towards the end, at 0:54, multiple frames within the frame feature different faces from the advert to show the range of styles and looks that have been showcased.

- The use of multiple shots in one scene borrows its iconography from social media and connotes community.
- A diverse range of people are shown using the make-up, connoting that the brand is for everyone.
- All shots are shown in close-up to allow the audience to see the transformative effect of the product.

> To remind yourself how to analyse mise en scène, review Chapter 2 of the Student Book.

Apply it

Choose a further three screenshots of your own from the advert.

Complete your own paragraph of mise en scène analysis for each one.

Social and cultural context

■ The relative nature of advertising and values and ideologies

To better understand how the advert conveys ideologies, look at this quote from Sephora senior marketing executive Abigail Jacobs (thedrum.com/creative-works/project/rga-sephora-black-beauty-beauty):

> Many of the trends we all participate in today, including acrylic nails, glitter, contouring and many more have roots in Black culture ... This is not widely known or celebrated. We believe that knowledge is a powerful tool and as such, as part of Sephora's overarching diversity and inclusion journey, wanted to leverage our platform and our beauty community to recognize and celebrate Black beauty, and invite everyone to participate in it.

From this, we can also understand how the brand attempts to counter potential damage from messaging that circulated prior to the advert's release. This included negative publicity about the brand on social media from black customers, who said they were followed by security in its shops and had to be conscious of their behaviour and the way they dressed to discourage this. Sephora's own marketing surveys supported this finding.

The quote also implies that:

- dominant ideologies about beauty do not correctly attribute beauty trends to their origins in black culture, or they ignore them
- previously this company (and possibly others) were not inclusive or diverse prior to this point (there has been a 'journey').

The notion of a journey signifies an acknowledgement by Sephora that it is responsive to social contexts and that the way in which it has historically addressed its target audience needs updating. Social media has given previously unheard voices more opportunity to challenge dominant ideologies in the media and this groundswell of voices makes issues more visible. These then move further up the representational agenda for brands, who cannot afford not to listen.

▲ This historical advertisement for Maybelline mascara demonstrates the dominant Westernised ideal of beauty standards as white

■ Narrative – constructing a story around the brand

The advertisement seeks to connect with a broader narrative about the hidden nature of black histories and cultural practices, which are under represented generally in the media. The voiceover is powerful in its construction of narrative about the role of black beauty in wider culture, informing the audience of the significance of this black contribution.

Todorov's theory can be applied to the advert, and it could be interpreted in terms of the way the brand wants to tell a story about its own journey in relation to its customer base:

- **Equilibrium**: the black experience is under-recognised within mainstream beauty culture.
- **Disruption**: the social and cultural climate has pushed black under-representations higher up the brand's agenda.
- **Recognition**: this could be in the decision to produce the 'short film'.

- **Attempt to repair**: noting numerous examples of the contributions made by black beauty to wider beauty culture.
- **New equilibrium**: the brand has repositioned black experiences more prominently within overall narratives about beauty.

Barthes' five codes can be used to explore the embedding of brand messages into storytelling in the advert. The following table gives one example of each of these – you could add more.

▼ Examples of Barthes' five codes applied to the Sephora advert

Hermeneutic codes	What contribution has black beauty made to beauty history?
Proairetic codes	Interaction between the voiceover and illustrative shots in sequence that demonstrate the technique referred to
Semantic codes	The mother tends to her daughter's hair, connoting bonding in beauty practices
Symbolic codes	Use of archive footage to illustrate black beauty history
Cultural/referential codes	Carnival preparations

Creating a desire for the product through narrative

Many advertisers use a model known as AIDA to inform their advertising strategy. This consists of the following stages:

- **Attention** – The brand uses the advert to gain the attention of the audience. This is accomplished at the beginning by showing women in what would usually be a quite private space in women's culture, a hair salon.
- **Interest** – The advert must maintain the audience's interest to fully decode the message. This is achieved using montage techniques and representation of an inclusive range of identities, both black and from other ethnicities. The voiceover acknowledges a range of accomplishments of black beauty icons and influences on broader beauty trends.
- **Desire** – The product must be made to seem desirable. Here, this is achieved by the inclusive and celebratory mode of address and positive representations of a wide range of people participating.
- **Action** – The audience should, if the advert has been successful, be able to participate in a range of actions. The advert closes with the line 'Join Sephora in supporting and celebrating black beauty' as a call to action. This might involve visiting a physical store or shopping online.

■ Techniques of persuasion

'Black Beauty is Beauty' signifies a shift in brand image on the part of Sephora, a French beauty brand whose market is global, to position itself as more inclusive. In 2019, the brand received complaints that it was racially profiling its customers. Sephora responded to this by offering increased diversity training to staff and conducting a radical overhaul of the way in which it positioned the brand.

The Sephora advert uses images of women from today and the past, allowing the viewer to peer into domestic spaces and beauty parlours, signifying the brand as everyday but simultaneously extraordinary in order to build a brand personality that feels approachable and relevant to black women.

Apply it
Explore how you can use structuralist theory, and specifically that by Lévi-Strauss, to examine the stories around the brand, including the role of make-up in identity and culture. Interestingly, the oppositional aspect of the reading can be felt in its addressing of a prior absence or lack of focus on the role of black beauty.

Quick question
Can you think of any binary oppositions that are present in the Sephora advert?

By crediting the role of black women in popularising certain tends and looks, it attempts to align the brand with these, making the brand the enabler of the looks people hope to create, including women from other ethnicities who make brief appearances in the advert.

Sound

The Sephora advert uses a pop disco beat in an unobtrusive commercial backing track. Disco is a popular form of dance music that first appeared in the 1970s and is commonly seen as the predecessor of many electronic and dance genres today. Many disco pioneers were black musicians and producers. The use of this music reinforces a message that black beauty's influence has been far-reaching and has become mainstream.

The voiceover, by an unseen black female narrator, addresses the audience with the lexical coding 'we', and speaks in an authoritative tone. This is strongly reminiscent of documentary as a media form.

Camerawork

Many of the long and medium shots in the advert have multiple subjects, emphasising the community and social aspects of beauty practices. The characters tend to be shot at eye level, to create a relationship between the audience and subjects, or with a slightly low angle, reinforcing their status and making them role models to look up to.

The two-shot of the mother and child reinforces the bonding experience of beauty traditions. Other shots include close-ups and extreme close-ups of make-up being applied or hair being styled, which allow techniques and details of influences to be clearly seen in a style reminiscent of make-up artist (MUA) tutorials.

Editing

The editing is fast-paced and allocates most of the screen time to featuring many different people. This allows the focus not to be on one person, but on a range of people with varied body types, skin tones and even gender using the products and techniques.

Split-screen effects are used at various points, which are very short in duration and replicate the codes of contemporary visual digital culture such as the Instagram grid and TikTok videos. These also signify that many people both contribute to black beauty techniques and can practise them. The effects emphasise community and connectedness.

The use of archive material – showing the legacy of black icons and the contribution of the entertainment industry and performers to popularising aspects of black beauty – is also a notable part of the editing, adding weight to the sense that black cultural histories are explored and promoted.

Representations

■ Stereotypes in cosmetic advertising

How advertisers make decisions about how to represent social groups can have far-reaching consequences for them, as we saw when exploring media language in the previous section. One of the areas that must receive careful consideration by today's producers is stereotyping.

The Sephora advert was directed by Garrett Bradley, a film-maker whose short films and documentaries often focus on the black experience and feature innovative storytelling techniques. Using a black woman, a member

> **Quick questions**
> 1. What are the four stages of the AIDA model used by many advertisers?
> 2. Explain in one sentence the effect of the voiceover in the Sephora advert.
> 3. Name two social media platforms that may have influenced the visual style of the editing.

of, typically, an out-group, is key to tone. Repositioning the brand using a representative of such a community means there is likely to be less repetition, conscious or otherwise, of the harmful stereotypes of black people we might see from the dominant in-group. This is achieved mainly through the range of different looks and people showcased by the advert.

There is a counter-argument to this, however. Most cosmetic and beauty advertisers primarily use young women in their campaigns, and this is still the case for the Sephora advert. It signifies powerfully that 'natural' beauty is not an ideal – that beauty is constructed through products and technology, not an innate quality of the women shown. This reinforces the patriarchal stereotype that women are expected to participate in high-maintenance beauty regimes to be attractive.

■ The advert as a version of reality

We know from the work of Stuart Hall that the media can only ever offer us a *version* of reality, a highly mediated version of the world. The Sephora advert seeks to encode ordinary black women as powerful owners of beauty history, innovators and trendsetters. It attempts to position the producers of the advert as champions in the promotion of black culture and supporting black women and businesses.

The advert, like all signs, is polysemic. The preferred reading of the advertisement is therefore of responsiveness to change, and of an inclusive and diverse agenda in marketing. An oppositional reading would find it to be nothing more than a virtue-signalling act of damage-limitation from a white-owned brand that has found itself as the subject of undesirable criticism on social media.

▲ **Garrett Bradley, director of the Sephora advert**

■ Representation and identity

David Gauntlett's ideas about identity and representation tell us that identity can be fluid and subject to revisions over time. For women, whose outward appearance is often an expression of identity, make-up and hair are particularly significant, and women will often look to representations in the media as a source of inspiration.

Social media and advertising can therefore be used as a way for people to negotiate their identity – to engage with specific role models as well as trends and fashions. This advert represents an effort on the part of Sephora as a brand to construct a collective identity – to make black women in particular seen and acknowledged as trailblazers in beauty techniques and practices.

■ Gender

We have already seen that the advert constructs beauty as being for anyone, including drag artists and other men. This is seen as more progressive if we consider Butler's work on the performative nature of gender. The application of a beauty regime could be read as the ultimate stylised repetition of a cultural act that traditionally encodes femininity; here, that role is more inclusive.

bell hooks' concern with intersectionality is also expressed in this advert – black women are quantitatively well represented, which is counter to mainstream beauty advertising. The opening shot depicts women in a beauty salon where different social classes may meet. Social class is almost made to disappear in this advert, which could form part of a negotiated or

Representations

even oppositional reading of it – that beauty transcends any other issues or obstacles faced by black women, who have been and often still are, marginalised.

Liesbet van Zoonen explores the way ownership and production roles in the media can be affected by gender. As a product made by a woman and for women, this advert neatly sidesteps accusations of distortion caused by male media producers representing women in conventional or stereotypical roles. In many ways, however, it does just that. Women are represented almost exclusively in domestic or entertainments settings, which many feminists of the past few decades would argue trivialises them as objects of the male gaze. On the other hand, Lyda Newman, who was a political activist and only the third black woman in the US to receive a patent (for her synthetic hairbrush), features briefly as an example of a black female inventor and pioneer.

■ Race and postcolonialism

Much of our focus so far in this CSP has been on how media language constructs race, as well as the significance of race to big brands in contemporary society. We can add to this by briefly exploring the ideas of Paul Gilroy.

Although produced primarily for a black US audience, we can read the advert as culturally syncretistic rather than absolutist, meaning it unites people from different countries with shared black experience of beauty culutre. Its message of black empowerment of women through beauty and promotion of hidden histories coincides well with the internationalised nature of black activism and awareness-raising of inequality. The double consciousness experienced by black women living in predominantly white countries in accessing beauty retailers is likely to be a global issue. The contribution of black women to mainstream beauty culture is something that majority white cultures will often not be aware of or recognise.

Wider contexts

■ Social context

It is important to read the advert while considering changing social attitudes to race and recognising the increasing awareness by brands that they need to broaden their appeal to minority groups in predominantly white markets such as the US, UK and the rest of Europe.

In 2020, Sephora signed up to the 'Fifteen Percent Pledge'. This is a commitment by companies to source 15 per cent (the percentage of the black population in the US) of their products from black-owned businesses and shows how big brands can respond with real action to pressure from social activists. Such responses can also be a challenge to get right and avoid being perceived by the audience as tokenistic.

■ Cultural context

Culturally, the advert draws on a hybrid of documentary and extended online advert forms and tries to acknowledge the contribution of black beauty to beauty culture in general. It addresses a young audience that is immersed in and familiar with the codes of hybridity of online forms.

> **Apply it**
>
> Do you believe that the Sephora advertisement is specifically American in its iconography, or is it transnational in its representation of black experience?
>
> Record your thoughts as a series of bullet points, using evidence from mise en scène to support your ideas.

> **Quick questions**
>
> 1. Name one way that Sephora sought to avoid stereotyping in their decisions about the advert's production.
> 2. Give and explain in one sentence an oppositional reading of the text in the advert.
> 3. Which black female inventor's work features in the advert?

Reaching out to digital natives online, where they may be consuming a range of other audiovisual content, shows recognition of the ways in which leisure time and popular media consumption have changed. Beauty advice and marketing used to take place primarily in magazines, but the internet has today become the preferred medium for women to source information about products and techniques.

The desire to look good on social media, and its globalised nature, has meant that beauty trends can spread fast, and this is recognised in the narrative of the advert.

> **Quick questions**
> 1 What is the Fifteen Percent Pledge?
> 2 What is the term used for the internet-savvy generation who are being targeted by the advert?
> 3 Which medium did women mainly use for their beauty information before the digital age?

Further reading

- 'How Sephora "hacked" Google search results to surface Black beauty', interesting article about wider aspects of the campaign strategy by the brand: marketingdive.com/news/sephora-black-beauty-google-search-results-rga/608589.
- 'Sephora celebrates Black beauty in new digital and TV campaign', short interview with representatives from Sephora and the advertising agency that produced the campaign: glossy.co/beauty/sephora-celebrates-black-beauty-in-new-digital-and-tv-campaign.
- 'Sephora and Target indicate support for Black-owned beauty brands', article about Sephora signing the Fifteen Percent Pledge: mintel.com/retail-market-news/sephora-and-target-indicate-support-for-black-owned-beauty-brands.

CSP 3 The Guardian

- **Platform:** print and online
- **Form:** newspaper and online site
- **Product:** *The Guardian* newspaper and website
- **Targeted elements of the theoretical framework:** audience and industry
- **Assessment information:** News may appear in Paper 1, Section B and could be assessed using a short-answer or long-answer question.

The study of *The Guardian* newspaper entails knowledge and understanding of its institutional structure and strategies to target a national and global readership as well as its position within the newspaper industry. You should be familiar with one complete print edition of the paper and two or more selected key pages from its website, including the homepage. The study of the digital presence of *The Guardian* is an important context for analysing the position of newspapers in the contemporary media landscape.

Industry

Britain's press (so called because newspapers were produced on a printing press) can trace its history back more than 300 years when William Caxton introduced the printing press to Britain in 1476. By the early sixteenth century, the first newspapers were seen in Britain. They were, however, slow to evolve, with the largely illiterate population relying on town criers and friends and family for news.

The first English daily newspaper, *The Daily Courant*, was launched in 1702, produced by Elizabeth Mallet from her home in London. The paper consisted of two sides of one sheet: one side was dedicated to foreign news and the other to advertisements. News production has changed dramatically and today is an endless 24/7 cycle of hard news – serious stories, such as politics or world events, and soft news – stories that blur the line between information and entertainment, such as a report about a celebrity.

■ The Guardian – a brief history

The Guardian has a long history. It began as The Manchester Guardian in 1821 before changing its name in 1959. Its founder was John Edward Taylor, a journalist who, along with other Manchester businessmen, funded the newspaper's creation after the 1819 Peterloo Massacre. At this event, 18 people died and between 400 and 700 injured when cavalry charged into a crowd of around 60,000 protestors who had gathered to demand the reform of representation in parliament. It outraged Taylor and others and compelled them to start a newspaper that could help to hold governments to account.

■ Ownership and control

News concentration refers to the level of ownership and control that a few media organisations have over the news industry. In the context of the UK, news concentration has been a topic of concern and debate due to the dominance of a small number of media conglomerates in shaping public discourse and influencing public opinion. It is argued that, in order for democratic societies to be pluralistic, there must be a wide variety of perspectives and viewpoints available to the population and, crucially, that news providers should not be influenced by governments and their policies. This concept is known as the free press. Over time, however, ownership and control of the British press has become concentrated in the hands of a few large conglomerates who control the majority of news production: News UK (owned by Rupert Murdoch's News Corp), Daily Mail and General Trust (DMGT) and Reach PLC.

Apply it

Take a look around the annotated, interactive first edition of The Guardian (then The Manchester Guardian) from Saturday 5 May 1821: theguardian.com/media/ng-interactive/2021/may/05/guardian-200-first-ever-edition-annotated.

- What new stories were making the headlines?
- How does the newspaper differ from your selected front page?

▼ Top three publishers by combined weekly circulation

Publisher	Weekly circulation	Share of total circulation
DMG Media	12.12m	42%
News UK	9.49m	33%
Reach	4.55m	16%

The Guardian ownership pattern differs as it is owned by the Guardian Media Group (GMG), which also owns The Observer and The Guardian Weekly. The parent company is the Scott Trust Ltd, which was established in 1936 to 'secure the financial and editorial independence of The Guardian' and to ensure that it is free from 'commercial or political interference'. This does not mean, however, that The Guardian is free from bias. As with any newspaper, it has institutional values that govern and shape its content. The Guardian is considered to be politically centre-left, adopting a 'critical friend' approach to the parties it is most aligned with – Labour, the Liberal Democrats and the Green Party – running many different types of article that both supports and critiques them. Much of the paper's content advocates for social and economic equality, fairness and justice, as well as protecting the environment and promoting diversity and inclusion. In a digital context, these topics have become increasingly appealing to audiences globally and GMG has expanded to include online editions for the US and Australia.

Industry

Editorial standards and self-regulation

The Guardian has formed its own regulatory board with *The Financial Times* and is not regulated by IPSO (Independent Press Organisation – the largest regulator of press and magazine content). *The Guardian* decided that the regulator was not independent enough and was not investigating breaches of journalistic standards such as accuracy, invasion of privacy and misrepresentation. It is the only British national daily to conduct an annual social, ethical and environmental audit (since 2003), in which it examines, under the scrutiny of an independent external auditor, its own behaviour as a company.

Other ways in which it upholds its editorial standards include *The Guardian US* creating a new editorial unit to investigate corporate and government misconduct, attacks on human rights and other urgent challenges facing the United States. According to a YouGov report in 2023, 'Which media outlets do Britons trust in 2023?' (YouGov is an international online research data and analytics technology group). *The Guardian* is the highest ranking non-business newspaper in terms of the highest trust figure.

Apply it

Visit *The Cotton Capital Chronicles* and read 'Slavery and the Guardian: the ties that bind us' at: theguardian.com/news/ng-interactive/2023/mar/28/slavery-and-the-guardian-the-ties-that-bind-us

How does this investigation into *The Guardian*'s ownership act as a form of regulation?

Quick question

In the context of news production, what does 'free press' refer to?

Apply it

The Guardian has faced a number of criticisms, such as exaggerating the effects of fake news and its discussion around trans rights. In an online context, other news outlets provide different viewpoints. For example, Double Down News (DDN), a left-wing media outlet funded by patrons, ran a video critiquing *The Guardian*'s reporting about Julian Assange, the former owner of WikiLeaks (a not-for-profit news database that published classified documents in 2006 to expose human rights violations).

Watch the video of Yanis Varoufakis talking about why the imprisonment of Julian Assange is negative for journalism: doubledown.news/watch/2023/october/6/they-want-to-kill-him-yanis-varoufakis-spoke-with-julian-assange.

- What does Varoufakis suggest *The Guardian*'s role was in relation to Julian Assange?
- How might this information be contrary to what you have learned about the newspaper?

The Guardian's funding model

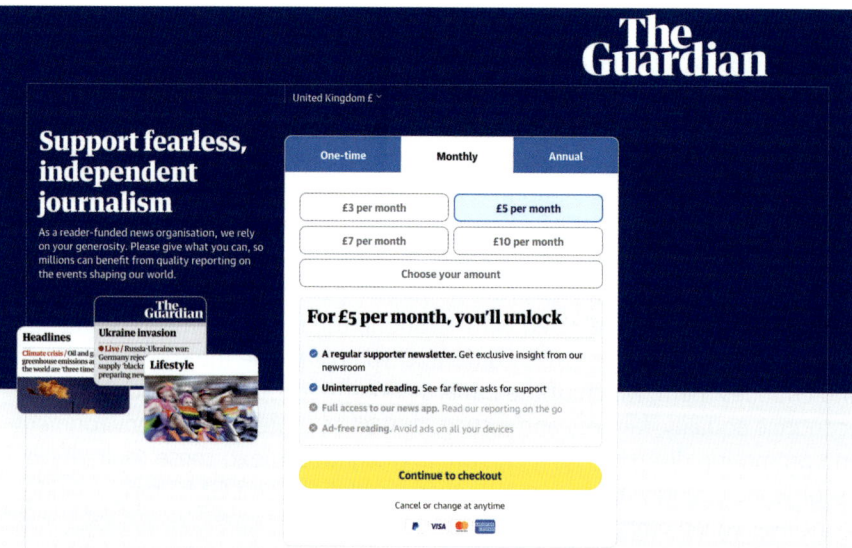

Funding news production is very expensive and, despite the seismic changes that the internet has brought to the news industry, *The Guardian* has been able to adapt when faced with declining print sales. It now finances its journalism through a combination of:

- printed newspaper sales
- digital subscriptions – the paper offers a range of packages to suit different economic groups
- patron support, with exclusive offers for those subscribing.
- philanthropic partnerships, such as with the Bill & Melinda Gates Foundation.

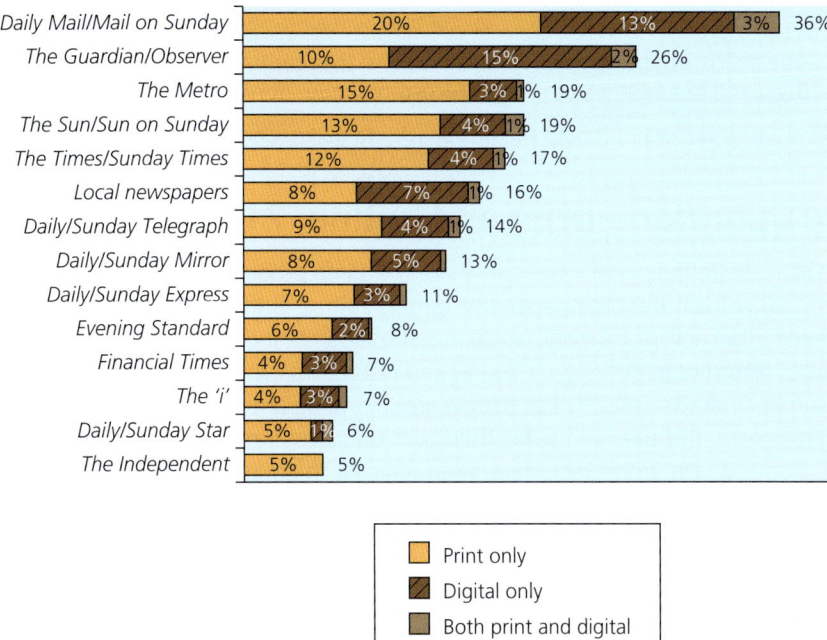

△ Ofcom's (Office of Communications) annual regulatory report into news consumption shows the growth of digital new over traditional print.

Almost all news institutions rely heavily on attracting advertisers, whether to their printed news products or their online site. It is a very competitive market where readership, circulation and online traffic figures are sold to advertisers. In this sense, news is a commodity, and the more attractive your news is to your audience the more visits you will get, which acts as an incentive for advertisers to pay to run their adverts. The website for *The Guardian* now has an average of 1.4 billion page views each month and 148 million unique browsers each month, on average, which offers advertisers a lot of potential customers.

Despite the importance of advertising, the news market is not as strong as it used to be, particularly in the UK. *The Guardian*'s subscription and patronage packages make up a substantial part of its revenue and more than a third of financial contributions come from readers in North America and Australia.

Apply it

The Guardian's Advertising Lab (advertising.theguardian.com/labs) is the branded-content wing of *The Guardian*, which dedicates itself to delivering branded content across various devices. The Guardian Labs reach 131 million unique browsers every month worldwide.

- Take a look the Advertising Lab. Write a mini case study of how it 'sells' itself to future advertisers.
- Look in your editions of the newspaper and online. Identify where you think there is partnership between *The Guardian* and brands.

Quick question

Define *The Guardian*'s institutional values and explain how they are apparent in a news story of your choice.

Apply it

Read the article about *The Guardian*'s revenues: theguardian.com/media/2023/jul/25/guardian-media-group-makes-record-revenues-for-news-business.

Make a list of factors that help the newspaper to make money.

The Guardian – print and online, 7 October 2023

The Guardian targets audiences that share the same progressive, liberal stance on current affairs, but the newspaper also targets culture enthusiasts, intellectuals, academics and activists. Broadly speaking, these come under the psychographic group of reformer as defined by Young and Rubicam's Cross-Cultural Consumer Characteristics. These people are said to be anti-materialist and seek enlightenment, but they also value their own opinions and judgements. The news stories on the front page have been selected to appeal to these readers, set the agenda on national news and encode the paper's institutional values.

△ Front page of *The Guardian*, Saturday 7 October 2023

CSP 3 THE GUARDIAN

■ Front page

The headline story is a hard news political report about the Labour Party winning a byelection in Rutherglen and Hamilton, but it is also a socio-economic story about the housing crisis in Scotland. 'Labour's new homes pledge' connotes them as trustworthy and the 'seismic byelection win' mediates them in a positive way and perhaps a party that can bring about change. This is a form of agenda-setting though selection. By interviewing Angela Rayner, the deputy leader of the Labour Party, about the pledge, the paper informs and potentially aligns those who read the article with the ideas. The interview uses lexis such as 'get tough' to construct a representation of Rayner as a resolute, fearless woman. Together with the other lead story about Narges Mohammadi winning the Nobel Peace Prize, this puts influential women, a minority group in terms of representation, on the front-page political and social agenda instead of the usual 'pale, stale and male' elites.

■ Inside stories

The story inside about Dale Vince, the green energy businessman pulling support for the activist group Just Stop Oil and funding the Labour Party for the next general election, acts as a form of anchorage on page 2 that keeps the audience's attention on Labour and its policies. The article, however, includes a range of information that juxtaposes three political ideologies on green issues: Labour announcing it will not permit any new oil or gas projects, the Conservative Party's U-turn away from various green initiatives, and a spokesperson from Just Stop Oil accusing Labour of 'tinkering around the edges while the world burns' and advocating direct action. This multi-perspective approach not only provides a broad overview of the issue but encourages the reader to judge which opinion they agree with.

Other stories in the newspaper cover social issues, such as police failing to protect children in London. Reports like this reflect *The Guardian*'s journalistic values of 'holding powerful institutions to account'.

There is also a skyline information panel on the front page that offer different gratifications for the reader. For example, 'Scams: All you need to know' offers surveillance needs (Blumler and Katz's uses and gratifications theory) and positions *The Guardian* as a watchdog for its readers. Arguably, these types of story act like clickbait does online: stories that include elements of danger and could potentially cultivate fear over time (Gerbner's mean world syndrome) and be used to sell news. Stuart Hall's reception theory, however, would argue that readers are not simply passive consumers of news but actively engage with media content, and this story could elicit a wide range of responses – fear being only one of them.

The skyline 'Bedbugs: How much to worry?' acts in a similar way and has possibly been selected because of its negative news value, which is said to interest audiences more than positive news. It is also humorous and light-hearted, constructing a wider variety of possible emotional responses from the reader and encouraging them to read (and buy) the newspaper. The DiCaprio opinion piece uses a rhetorical question, 'Activist hero?', in the skyline, appeal to readers' intellectual curiosity and invites them to cultivate their own conclusions.

The Guardian – print and online, 7 October 2023

Inside the newspaper, there are many stories that enhance cultural capital (Pierre Bordieu). For example, 'Eyewitnesses of the week' is a series of photojournalist images that cover a wide range of topics, such as judges arriving at Westminster and migrants travelling to Mexico from Venezuela. These are likely to appeal to the intellectual and aesthetic needs of the reader – a key characteristic of the reformer category.

> ### Apply it
> Using the edition you are studying, identify stories that reflect the areas in the table below.
> - How does the newspaper present the issues – negatively or positively?
> - What does this suggest about *The Guardian*'s viewpoints on these issues?
> - What potential effects could this have on audiences?

Story	Example	Institutional values and interest to audience
Politics and politicians		
Corporate power		
War and conflict		
Social class: poverty, housing and cost of living		
Race, diversity and multi-culturalism		
Gender issues; women, identity		
Education	'Warning over unconscious bias against working-class pupils in English schools' (theguardian.com/society/2023/oct/03/warning-unconscious-bias-working-class-pupils-schools-england). Combines political, education and social class issues, which figure highly in *The Guardian*'s reporting remit. Especially critical of how working-class young people are referred to as 'disadvantaged' – a term that labels them as inadequate and is said to create unconscious bias against them.	Social justice stories appeal to *Guardian* readers. Educators may also be interested and could reflect on their own practice after reading the article.
Celebrity		

■ Online edition

In the increasingly competitive landscape of online news *The Guardian* online has become the third largest individual newspaper website in the world, delivering news to over 62 million unique browsers worldwide every month, with almost two-thirds of these coming from outside the UK. Like the printed paper, the online site is aimed at liberal progressives, but it has huge scope, offering content that would appeal to a wide variety of readers beyond its target demographic.

It has UK, US and Australian editions (which can be accessed by adding /uk, /us or /au after its main URL: theguardian.com/). The UK site is organised into sections for ease of selection, for example:

- News
- Headlines
- Spotlight
- Opinion
- Sport
- Newsletters
- Climate crisis
- Tip us off
- Take part
- Explore
- In pictures
- Culture
- Lifestyle
- Video
- Opinion
- Editorials and Letters
- From the UK
- Around the world
- Most viewed
- In pictures

The site makes use of technological convergence, with multimedia content such as podcasts, videos, documentaries and interactive elements. The site can be updated in real time and respond to critical events immediately, for instance with various live blogs following developing stories, such as a political speech or vote. In a digital age, this can be positive and negative for journalism: content can be bundled-up easily and transformed to fit different digital platforms much quicker than it could be presented in the past, but it is hard to fact-check thoroughly in time.

Journalists often use information from a multitude of sources, including social media sites like X (Twitter), to quote directly from those involved. Live reporting and timeline mapping keep readers up to date with critical events, like the wars in Ukraine and Israel/Gaza.

The Guardian also produces visual and interactive journalistic content that covers issues from 'where to buy a house' to how air pollution is 'damaging every organ in the body'. Unlike in the past, when news institutions had very little contact with their consumers, *The Guardian* has multiple ways to establish feedback loops with its readers, such as polls, surveys and questionnaires.

One such example was when readers wanted to know how to distinguish between a straight news report and an analysis. The result was 'analysis' being clearly labelled to distinguish fact from opinion or interpretation: a direct response to reader interaction. This is an example of readers being engaged with news in an active way, along with various articles that have commenting available on them that demonstrate many different 'receptions' (Stuart Hall) to the written content.

> **Quick question**
> What is the difference between technological convergence and cultural convergence?

> **Apply it**
> Go to *The Guardian's* YouTube channel: youtube.com/@theGuardian. Select two stories which interest you and discuss the following:
>
> - What were your responses to the stories?
> - What different gratifications do they offer in comparison to a print edition?
> - How does a multi-media approach to news develop the brand of *The Guardian*?

The Guardian – print and online, 7 October 2023

CSP 4: Blinded by the Light

- **Platform:** cinema industry
- **Form:** film production, marketing and distribution
- **Product:** independent film release of *Blinded by the Light*
- **Targeted elements of the theoretical framework:** For your exam, you will study the film's production, distribution and circulation context in terms of media industries. There is no textual study of the film or requirement to have seen it. Your focus will be on production and distribution materials including Warner Bros, the website for Bend It Networks, and the trailer and posters for the film. The economic, social and cultural contexts are also studied.
- **Assessment information:** In the exam, questions about *Blinded by the Light* will appear in Section B of Paper 1. There is no second close study product for film industries. You may be asked either a shorter question or a longer, 20-mark question based on this study.

Blinded by the Light is a film by British director Gurinder Chadha released in 2019. The film is loosely based on the book *Greetings from Bury Park: Race, Religion, Rock 'n' Roll*. Its author, journalist Sarfraz Manzoor, also co-wrote the script with Chadha.

Industry

The making of the film – a low-to-mid-budget release

The film's production was a collaboration between Bend It Films (now known as Bend It Networks), Levantine Films and Ingenious Media. Gurinder Chadha, the film's director, has made nine films since 1993. Most of them feature characters who are British Asians, an underrepresented community in British media generally.

▼ Film companies that collaborated to produce *Blinded by the Light*

Bend It Networks	London-based production company owned by Chadha and her US-born partner, screenwriter Paul Mayeda Berges. The company has diversified into stage and television production and aims to 'take stories of characters who are normally on the margins and place them at the centre of the screen for mainstream, international audiences' (benditnetworks.com/about).
Levantine Films	US-based production company that finances its own film productions. The mission statement on its website homepage states its commitment to 'Developing and financing compelling, character-driven stories that entertain, spark conversation and bring awareness to underrepresented segments of society.' It emphasises that, despite this less mainstream focus in content, it backs projects that are 'commercially viable' (levantine-films.com/get-to-know-us).
Ingenious Media	UK investment company that raises capital through a range of projects, including property as well as media. This diversification into more than one market gives the company more flexibility in choosing what to invest in, since it lessens risk overall. 'We believe that our investments should deliver not only for our investors but also create a positive impact for the communities in which we operate' (theingeniousgroup.co.uk).

In many ways, the film is characteristic of a low-to-mid-budget release. Gurinder Chadha's name and track record of producing relatively successful films means that these companies were likely to see a return for their investment, in this case on a production budget of $15 million.

The collaboration of several production companies from different parts of the world is common in the UK film and television industry, where budgets on the whole are smaller but require collaboration to raise sufficient investment to make a film that can compete in a global market. In the US, by comparison, the Hollywood studio system is often vertically integrated, where a single corporation may see a film through from production to circulation.

■ The role of Bruce Springsteen's music

Bruce Springsteen had read the book that the film is based on. When approached by Manzoor and Chadha, he immediately lent his support to the project. This paved the way for the inclusion of 12 of his songs on the soundtrack. His approval was gained at each step of the project, including the final script.

Springsteen's music gave the film more appeal in the US in particular, but Springsteen's reach as a rock star is global and played an important role in ensuring press attention for the film's release in the UK and other countries too.

■ Film festivals and distribution

Film festivals can play an important role for independent film-makers in gaining a distribution deal. *Blinded by the Light* premiered at the renowned Sundance Film Festival in the US and gained one of the biggest distribution deals of the festival, at $15 million, from New Line Cinema (owned by Warner Bros). Distribution rights in the UK were purchased by a separate Canadian company, eOne Entertainment, which has now been bought by Lionsgate.

■ Traditional marketing techniques

Films today continue to use traditional film marketing methods, even though these are comparatively expensive compared with the types of new media distribution used for advertising.

Some traditional marketing methods include the techniques in the following table. These have not yet been supplanted by contemporary methods, but some digital marketing methods are comparatively cheaper and can extend the reach of a film with a lower marketing budget.

As is often the case with international film releases, the marketing may change depending on the region where the film is being advertised. For example, posters for the UK were predominantly orange, a bright, cheerful colour. The US posters made greater use of the lead character's dress code that signifies his attachment to Springsteen and reflects colours of the US flag, seen as patriotic.

▼ Film marketing techniques

Traditional marketing method	New digital strategy
Interviews with cast or crew in printed film magazines and on TV entertainment news	Online content creation and short-form video for social media
Trailers in cinemas	Trailers on online platforms
Posters, on billboards, buses and outside cinemas	Digital posters, banners and web ads

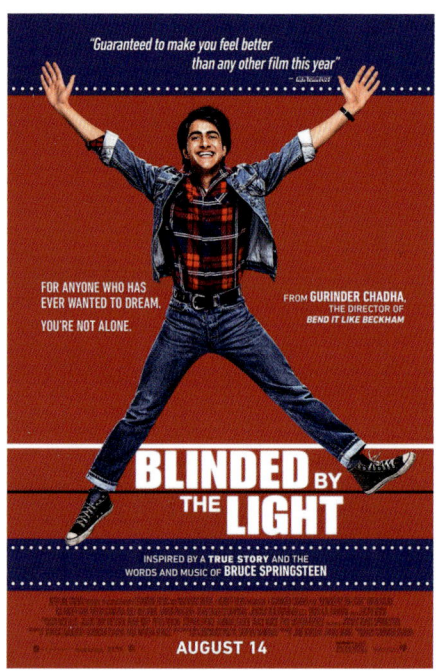
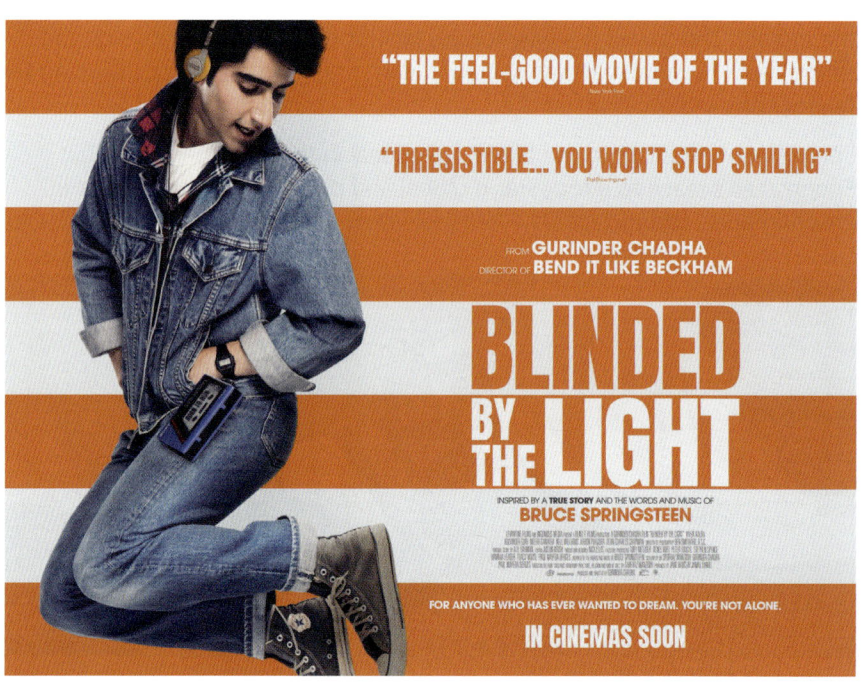

▲ These images show some subtle differences between the marketing of the film in the US (left) and that in the UK (right)

■ Other marketing techniques

Blinded by the Light is primarily a coming-of-age film, a popular genre that often focuses on a turning point in a young person's life and barriers they must overcome. Coming-of-age narratives have a universal appeal that travels well globally, regardless of the cultural context of the setting. A film such as *Blinded by the Light* can resonate with British Asians, and the diaspora of South Asian families internationally, who have pleasure in seeing their lived experiences on screen, but there are many other ways in which people from different ethnicities may relate to the issues of youth and identity formation that go beyond race.

Other qualities that contribute to the film's generic hybridity, and therefore wide appeal, include the influence of music videos and musical and comedy films.

The setting of the film in the 1980s has currency for the film-makers by tapping into cultural nostalgia. This era arouses the curiosity of young people as the last time we were without digital technology in daily use and is often evoked as a simpler time. For older audience members, there is the pleasure of reliving an era they remember, and their own youth.

Apply it

Watch the trailer for the film (youtube.com/watch?v=f1YFA_J5JBU).

Explore how it signifies some of the marketing techniques looked at earlier in its selection of content from the film.

New technologies and distribution – VoD and streaming

New technologies have significantly impacted the revenue that can be made from sales of hard copies of the film on physical media such as DVD. Film lovers today are more likely to stream a film, regardless of whether they rent or buy it. This means that the film can continue to make money long after it departs the cinema. This is known as the long-tail effect.

Blinded by the Light made $18.1 million at the box office, a modest performance compared with many Hollywood films, but it will continue to accrue revenue if its presence is maintained on the following or other platforms. According to the Warner Bros website at the time of writing, the film is available to buy or rent from:

- Apple TV
- Google Play
- YouTube
- Prime Video
- VUDU
- Movies Anywhere
- Microsoft
- FandangoNow.

New technologies have also impacted the ways in which films are marketed – social media has become a vital part of strategy. The Instagram account for the film (@blindedbythelightfilm) is a good example, carrying numerous clips as reels (short video clip/montage), posters, snippets of interviews and some dedicated social media adverts. For instance, one reel from 8 August 2019 promotes the film by scrolling down a pile of cassette tapes that present the film and its makers as well as featuring mix tapes that introduce the lead characters.

Regulation of the industry by the BBFC

Film releases in the UK are regulated by the British Board of Film Classification (BBFC). Under UK law, cinemas and film distributors must not supply a film in retail, rental, or cinema outlets to people under the age stated and have a duty to enforce this. At home, it is up to parents to make decisions about the suitability of a film's content. Age ratings can help with this decision.

Blinded by the Light received a 12 certificate for depictions of racist behaviour and language and moderate bad behaviour. A better understanding of the factors involved in regulation may be gained by exploring the criteria that inform the certificate.

Lunt and Livingstone's work suggests that regulating any media product is always a balance between protecting the rights of the consumer to access entertainment they feel is appropriate for them and their family, and allowing them to make informed judgements about this as citizens. Parents want to feel protected by age certificates, reassured that these will pre-filter suitable content for their children, but reserve the right to make their own decisions about individual films in their own homes.

Apply it

To explore film age certification, visit the BBFC website at bbfc.co.uk/rating/12.

Look at the key points that describe what must be taken into account when certificating a film as suitable for audiences aged 12 or above.

- Consider how far these standards serve to protect the citizen.
- Can you connect these ideas with either social learning theory or cultivation effects to consider why they might be useful in categorising film content?

> **Quick questions**
> 1 Name three aspects of *Blinded by the Light* that contribute to its marketing potential.
> 2 What are the main characteristics of a 12-certificate film?
> 3 Which three main production companies worked together to create sufficient investment to get *Blinded by the Light* made?

Contexts

■ Economic context

Blinded by the Light presents us with a peculiarly British location and context – a British Asian coming of age in Luton during Prime Minister Margaret Thatcher's 1980s – but successfully creates from this an internationalised product due to its use of the universal coming-of-age theme and the work of a global music icon. It embodies the ways in which British cultural industries are dependent to some extent on support from globalised industrial practices in terms of production, distribution and circulation.

■ Social and cultural contexts

The film also draws on British social realism, a film-making tradition that may be niche and culturally specific but is often critically well received. Social realist dramas often feature ordinary working-class characters and their social struggles such as racism. The themes of poverty, unemployment and racism set in the time of Prime Minister Margaret Thatcher have additional resonance for the British audience without alienating global audiences. However, unlike many social realist films that are very bleak to the end, *Blinded by the Light* is marketed as a 'feel good film' and provides us with a happy ending, making it much more accessible to mainstream audiences.

Gurinder Chadha continues to highlight the lack of female directors in the film industry. In one interview about the distribution deal gained at Sundance, she highlights that almost 50 per cent of the films selected for Sundance in the same year as *Blinded by the Light* were directed by women – an unusually high number. The Celluloid Ceiling is a research group that tracks the roles of women in top US films, from cast to crew. In 2019, they found that only 12 per cent of directors of the 100 top-grossing films in the US were female.

> **Quick questions**
> 1 Which British tradition in film-making does *Blinded by the Light* borrow from in part?
> 2 Which aspect of British society that the film portrays would be powerful for British audiences who lived through the 1980s?
> 3 What was unique about the films selected for Sundance in 2019?

Further reading

The *Close Study Products* booklet provides a wide range of useful links, and you should explore all of these during your study of the product. In addition, the 2019 Celluloid Ceiling report, 'Behind-the-Scenes Employment of Women on the Top 100, 250, and 500 Films of 2019', may be helpful: womenintvfilm.sdsu.edu/wp-content/uploads/2020/01/2019_Celluloid_Ceiling_Report.pdf.

CSP 5 *Newsbeat*

- **Platform**: radio
- **Form**: audio media
- **Product**: *Newsbeat* cross-platform news content
- **Targeted elements of the theoretical framework**: audience and industries, the social and cultural contexts. This CSP is paired with the famous 1938 US radio broadcast *The War of the Worlds*. You will not be required to conduct any textual analysis of the programmes. However, to become familiar with the product, it is strongly recommended you listen to some episodes and explore the various ways in which *Newsbeat* features across the BBC's digital platforms and other places such as social media.
- **Assessment information**: Radio questions are answered in Section B of Media One. You could be required to answer a shorter question only on *Newsbeat* or a longer response worth 20 marks in which you compare aspects of it and *The War of the Worlds*.

Newsbeat, a scheduled news broadcast, was launched on Radio 1 in September 1973, in response to competition from commercial radio stations. The latter were widely seen as being better at addressing a youth audience in terms of the accessibility and style of their news bulletins.

Today, *Newsbeat* can be heard as scheduled broadcasts on the radio, streamed online or listened to as a podcast on BBC Sounds. It has also diversified into short-form news articles on the BBC website and short video content on YouTube and other social media channels. For this reason, *Newsbeat* is defined as a 'transitional' media product as it continues to be broadcast traditionally as well as through other digital methods.

Industries

■ *Newsbeat* as part of the BBC's news offering

Newsbeat is 'simulcast' (simultaneously broadcast) over three radio stations – Radio 1, 1Xtra and Asian Network. These three stations have a predominantly youth audience, so require a different style and presentation from the BBC's other news services. Other examples of BBC news programming include a 24-hour news television channel available on Freeview and in-depth reporting of news and current affairs such as the three-hour morning broadcast of *Today* on Radio 4.

■ The funding of BBC Radio

BBC Radio is funded by the licence fee (known in the UK as the TV licence), a hypothecated tax. This means that the money raised by its payment is used only for a specific purpose, in this case funding public service broadcasting. The licence is paid by all UK households that have equipment with which they can receive BBC content, regardless of whether they claim to use these services or not, with the exception of some groups such as pensioners.

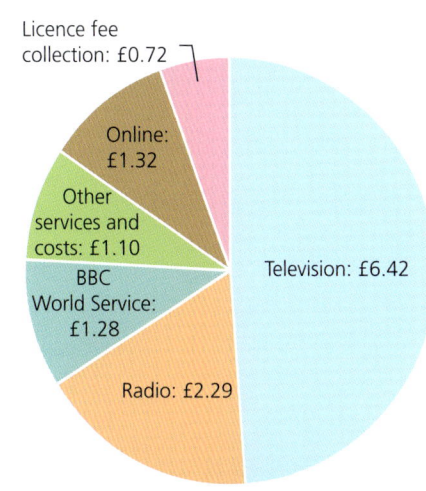

▲ Where the monthly 2020–21 BBC licence fee was spent

The public service broadcaster in the contemporary media landscape

The position of the BBC in the UK as a public service broadcaster is perhaps unique compared with other countries in terms of the high profile enjoyed historically by BBC services compared with commercial stations and channels. Because it is funded by the licence fee, the BBC has, for many years, been able to offer comparatively well-funded content that is able to compete with commercial offerings without the requirement to carry advertising.

Today, this role is becoming more challenging. A globalised media market has meant an increase in competition from content on the web and other media services. Podcasting and the convenience of streaming internet radio fragment the existing audience of radio listeners still further.

In addition, *Newsbeat*'s listeners have a wide range of other multimedia content to consume, with the BBC's offering challenged by social media, gaming and platforms such as YouTube. All of this means the future of the licence fee may be in doubt, as this younger audience ages and begins to question more the mandatory payment of a hypothecated tax for a service it uses less and less.

Catering for a youth audience

The main provision of the BBC for a youth audience on radio are the stations Radio 1, 1Xtra and Asian Network, all of which broadcast *Newsbeat*. It thus reaches listeners from diverse ethnic backgrounds. The presentation of news is fundamental in attracting a youth audience, and approximately 8 million listeners hear *Newsbeat* every week in the UK. (These factors are considered more closely in the audiences section, later.)

Right from its inception, *Newsbeat* has focused on the issues of the day that would interest its younger audience. Its use of upbeat jingles and background music, content that suits their interests and a snappy, fast mode of address influenced by American and Australian radio was distinctive and new when it began. *Newsbeat*'s editorial team used clips and soundbites in preference to long interviews, making the news easier to digest.

Today, *Newsbeat* has had to diversify its news formats across digital platforms to ensure it reaches younger listeners who are digital natives.

Public service remit

The BBC's mission is defined as: 'to act in the public interest, serving all audiences through the provision of impartial, high-quality and distinctive output and services which inform, educate and entertain' (bbc.com/aboutthebbc/governance/mission).

The last words – *inform*, *educate* and *entertain* – have remained central to the BBC's purpose since its formation in 1922 under the leadership of John Reith. *Newsbeat* sits well with this mission – it informs its audience, educates them about relevant current affairs and social issues, and presents the news in a format that entertains.

The Royal Charter of the BBC identifies a range of public purposes of the organisation. The first of these relates directly to news production: 'to provide impartial news and information to help people understand and engage with the world around them'. This is further explained as requiring accuracy and impartiality in its news, a good depth of analysis and freedom of expression.

Apply it

Read the full explanation of the first purpose from the BBC's public purposes as listed on its website: bbc.com/aboutthebbc/governance/mission.

Using this statement, along with two *Newsbeat* broadcasts of your choice, write a short report – around 200 words – explaining how the content of the bulletins fulfils the purpose of providing impartial news and helping people to understand and engage with the world around them. Include reference to:

- accuracy and impartiality
- helping to build understanding of all parts of the UK and wider world
- using high-calibre journalists and presenters
- championing freedom of expression
- allowing audiences to engage with local and global issues
- encouraging participation in the democratic process as active, informed citizens.

Newsbeat as a multi-platform product

Newsbeat has a strong cross-platform presence, not only being broadcast as a traditional scheduled programme but also producing branded video content and traditional written journalism with a more relaxed mode of address than a standard online news article.

An estimated 14 million views are made each week of *Newsbeat*'s online content. For example, on 16 June 2022, *Newsbeat* posted on its Facebook page a short video featuring *Love Island* contestant Demi Jones and former *Hollyoaks* actress Abi Phillips. The video showed a meeting between the two in which they discuss their experiences of being treated for thyroid cancer. The video educates the audience in an accessible way about symptoms, diagnosis and treatment, and gets across a public health message using celebrity role models who speak candidly to each other rather than to the audience, borrowing from a mode of address common to reality television.

Newsbeat also runs a YouTube channel in addition to its website presence and other social media accounts. This allows a broader reach than traditional radio and is essential for a transitional media product that must try to bridge both traditional media and the multi-platform, post-broadcast era of the digital age.

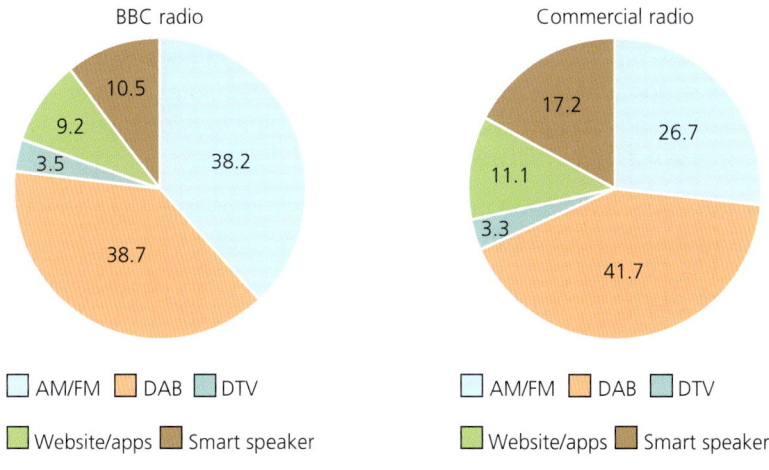

△ Listener survey results from RAJAR (Radio Joint Audience Research–the radio audience monitoring organisation), which show the diverse ways in which audiences today might access radio

■ The regulation of the BBC

The BBC is regulated by both Ofcom and, to an extent, its own governance, the BBC Board. The Royal Charter is the constitutional basis of the work done by the BBC and underpins its agreement and mission to serve the public in the UK. The BBC Board also ensures that the BBC performs its duty as a form of self-regulation, although the regulatory authority rests with Ofcom.

The most significant aspect of Ofcom's regulatory role in relation to news consumption is its role in regulating programme content. If someone is dissatisfied with some aspect of *Newsbeat*'s content, they can make a report via Ofcom's website, and Ofcom is then obligated to investigate it.

It is also possible to complain directly to the BBC about issues of fairness, bias, factual inaccuracy, or any other aspect of news. This demonstrates that a strong culture of journalistic self-regulation is also in place to maintain editorial standards. The BBC's internal complaints department will investigate any complaint about a news article made through its website within two to three weeks and provide a response directly to each individual complaint.

> **Quick questions**
> 1 What do we mean when we say the licence fee is a hypothecated tax?
> 2 Which three key words are associated with the BBC's public service remit?
> 3 Which organisation regulates radio in the UK?

Audiences

■ Techniques used to reach a youth audience

Newsbeat has its own studios and presenting team that are now based in Birmingham, which was part of the BBC's redistribution of content production around the UK to regions such as Salford, Bristol and Glasgow from London. The team focuses on content that addresses a youth audience, offering current affairs in terms these people are likely to engage with. The recent rebranding and regular updating of the programme music keep the programme feeling fresh and relevant.

The selection of content that is appealing, coupled with a less formal mode of address, leads to a much more participatory style of news broadcasting. Comments from listeners are read out live in a style that can feel more like a conversation than a formal news broadcast.

Debbie Ramsay, then long-standing editor of *Newsbeat*, said in a 2019 interview (mediamasters.fm/debbie-ramsay):

> *It's about your tone, and about just not treating people as idiots really, just because they might not get a certain topic, or understand a really long word, like 'superfluous' or something. You just don't use it. It's cut out the jargon and talk to people simply as you would to a mate really; whatever age you are, you don't talk to a mate in jargon, you just talk to them as a normal person.*

This intention to present the news in an accessible way continues to resonate throughout *Newsbeat*'s multi-platform presence today.

Presentation style

A notable feature of the broadcast that allows it to retain pace and still feel part of the music broadcast is the use of dedicated jingles, which precede the broadcast and signify its start and continue quietly in the mix during the presentation of the features. The music, which was once updated annually, is now changed less frequently, meaning that a new jingle becomes a participatory point of comment itself. Different jingles signify different parts of the broadcast – news, sport, weather – helping the broadcast to feel pacy and lively.

> To listen to the current (since 2022) *Newsbeat* music and understand how it addresses a youth audience, visit youtube.com/watch?v=Pfa1ZOIDSJM, where you can hear listener comments on the new jingle being referred to by the presenter at 3:53.

News values

News values – the reasons why something is considered news – can tell us a great deal about the interests of a specific audience. They are used by news providers to target audiences in a way that promotes specific ideologies in keeping with their news agenda, and to make use of content that matches their audiences' needs. In the case of the BBC, the news agenda is informed not by political bias or ownership, but by its mission and public purposes.

News values to be found in all news media are:

- **negativity** – bad news
- **proximity** – news from close to home (domestic: national or local)
- **currency** – how well it fits with other events
- **continuity** – whether there will be more to report on
- **simplicity** – how easy it is to understand, used frequently in *Newsbeat*
- **personality** – soft news, such as relating to celebrity culture, used frequently in *Newsbeat*
- **uniqueness** – surprising or unexpected events
- **expectedness** – predictable, diary events that happen on publicised dates
- **elite nations and people** – the powerful in the world (often Western nations and influential people, or those seen as a threat to them, may be disproportionately reported on)
- **exclusivity** – special access to certain people or news
- **threshold** – how many people it affects.

The more of these news values a story hits, the more likely it is to move up a news agenda or appear closer to the start of a bulletin. From this list, we can see that *personality* and *simplicity* are likely to be frequently used news values. *Proximity* could also be interpreted as relevant to a youth audience – does the story affect young people disproportionately in the population?

Content selection

One of the best ways to explore content selection for *Newsbeat* is to look online at the selected stories on a given day as well as listening to a 15-minute lunchtime broadcast. This gives a clearer idea of the way in which *Newsbeat* selects its stories to match the interests of the target audience. For example, in online news on 10 October 2023, the following stories featured:

- shortages in ADHD medication and how these are affecting young people
- an article about TikTok and film soundtracks
- a focus on the use of Arabic language in the game *Assassin's Creed*
- an interview with singer Olivia Rodrigo
- tackling barriers in women's football
- a guide to the Cricket World Cup
- an article about AI and songwriting
- a retrospective on the life of rapper Tupac Shakur
- an interview with a Eurovision contestant.

These stories demonstrate the strong links the programme has with popular music. It has a clear way to engage an audience already listening to music-dominated content when the bulletin is broadcast and constructs the audience as having a strong interest in a range of music. Mental health issues, gender equality and other aspects of popular culture such as computer games, films and technological advances are also relevant.

> **Apply it**
>
> Visit the *Newsbeat* webpage at bbc.co.uk/news/newsbeat and choose a single broadcast episode.
>
> - Listen to the broadcast and write down the individual stories. Note how these have been selected for their appeal to a youth audience.
> - Apply news values to these same stories.

Audiences

■ Audience interaction, participation and self-representation

Audience members respond to *Newsbeat* by various digital communications and their comments are sometimes included in bulletins. Listeners are encouraged to contact the programme using social media or email. The conversational mode of address, coupled by the intimacy of radio as a medium, give the feeling of a social relationship with presenters.

Newsbeat also fosters a sense of participation and representation by featuring 'citizen journalist' pieces online by people who have had experience of an issue in the news such as mental health problems, youth unemployment and so on.

■ Demographics and psychographics

Radio 1's demographic is identified by the BBC as aged 15 to 29, although demographic research by RAJAR consistently shows many listeners to be in the upper end of this age bracket. Stories selected by *Newsbeat* cover a range of issues likely to appeal to both genders. The simulcast of the programme on 1Xtra and Asian Network means that a range of ethnicities are also directly targeted, with praise having been given by the audience for coverage of stories relating to countries such as India and Pakistan that often don't make it as high as 'elite' nations on the news agenda of other programmes.

Since Radio 1 is a mainstream broadcaster for a youth audience, we could assume that many of the listeners will fit a mainstreamer psychographic profile, with many young people who have a love of fashion and music also being aspirers and/or reformers. This is a diverse audience to please, and *Newsbeat* achieves this by sticking to an agenda highly relevant to the youth market and creating an upbeat sound to even the most serious of news stories and mixing these with softer news.

> For more about psychographics, a blog post from B2B Marketing provides an excellent introduction: b2bmarketing.net/feature-post-b2b-insights/psychographics-the-b2b-marketers-latest-greatest-bff-or-it-should-be-part-i.

△ Designer James Mobbs working on the BBC's most recent rebrand of *Newsbeat*, which takes into account its youth audience as well combining existing colour codes from the three main radio stations that carry the bulletins

Cultivation theory

A cultivation effect can be found in the increase in the 'mean world' index of news consumption. The more hours that are spent listening to or consuming news, there is a theoretical likelihood that a greater cultivation effect will occur. The main result of hearing overwhelmingly negative news is mean world syndrome, where audiences believe the world to be a more dangerous place.

There can also be a social learning effect on some listeners to news. Activism, for example, might come about because of people's galvanisation by a particular situation in the news.

The BBC is often accused of political bias by both audiences and politicians, most often of being too 'liberal'. However, since a public purpose is to cater for everyone in the UK, there is a stronger emphasis on the selection of news about minority groups and issues, such as gender equality or gay rights, than might be found on some news services.

Mainstreaming through the news means that a programme such as *Newsbeat* can contribute to the democratic process by offering balanced reporting of political issues, perhaps encouraging a generation of younger listeners to vote and feel informed about and engaged with political issues. For example, *Newsbeat*'s lunchtime broadcast on 10 October 2023 focused on both the content of a speech given by Labour Party leader Keir Starmer and a protester's interruption of it.

Coverage of current affairs that is meaningful to a youth audience will also allow that audience to experience resonance, reinforcing their perceptions of the news source as reliable since it engages with aspects of their own lives.

Reception theory

We know that, according to Stuart Hall's model, people may differ in their conceptual maps and read news stories differently. Life experience, political viewpoints and many other factors shape our responses to news. Even a product as simple as a news broadcast may be read as polysemic and is open to a range of interpretations from the hegemonic to the oppositional.

For example, one listener might be appreciative of *Newsbeat*'s slightly longer and more in-depth coverage of a flare-up of conflict in the Middle East and feel informed by it. Another listener might find that the abrupt transition from a report of an attack by Hamas on Israeli territory to coverage of a porridge-making competition trivialises people's suffering in the region and the conflict itself (as was the sequence on *Newsbeat*, 10 October 2023).

> **Quick questions**
> 1. What is the purpose of a simulcast as a broadcasting strategy?
> 2. What demographic is identified by the BBC as the target age of its listeners?
> 3. Give two examples of factors that might shape our reception of news products.

Cultural and social significance

Social context

The shape of news consumption is changing hugely for young people in the 16 to 24 age group that forms a large part of *Newsbeat*'s target audience. Ofcom research into news consumption in 2022 found that only 20 per cent of this group gained their news from radio, in comparison with 40 per cent of other adults. This makes the role of *Newsbeat* even more socially significant as a source of balanced and objective reporting on issues, particularly since 83 per cent of this group are accessing their news online, compared with 68 per cent of the rest of the adult population.

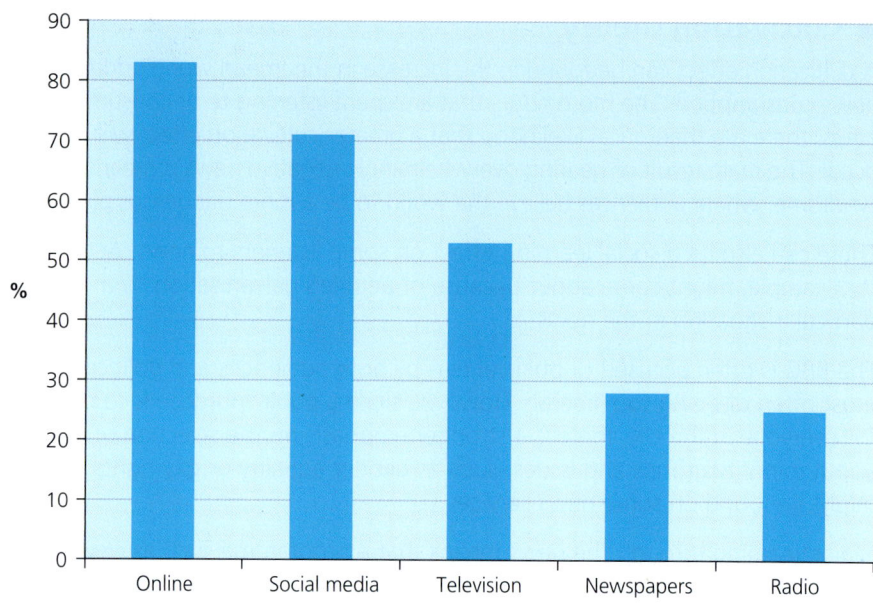

▲ A breakdown of how young people aged 16–24 source their news 16–24 age bracket when consuming news online, and where they get it from

■ Cultural context

The BBC has a high status in the UK as a respected news provider as well as being considered reliable and scoring highly on trust as a news source. BBC products are associated nationally with quality news provision and its services are often regarded fondly by audiences as part of British identity. The BBC brand is recognised worldwide and has one of the highest statuses internationally of any public service broadcaster.

Further reading

- Website for the Radio Joint Audience Research, an excellent source of information for general listening and station statistics: rajar.co.uk/index.php.
- Full explanation of the BBC's mission and public purposes: bbc.com/aboutthebbc/governance/mission.
- Explanation of Ofcom's role in regulating the BBC: bbc.com/aboutthebbc/governance/regulation.
- In-depth interview with former *Newsbeat* editor Louise Ramsay: mediamasters.fm/debbie-ramsay.

CSP 6 — Zendaya's social media

- **Platform**: online, social and participatory media
- **Form**: social media. Online media is an in-depth media form, so the products should be analysed using ideas from all four areas of the theoretical framework: media language, representation, audience and industry.
- **Product:** Zendaya's social media presence, including her website and Instagram, X and Facebook accounts.
- **Assessment information**: You could be asked to discuss Zendaya's social media in Paper 2. You will also need to study the online newspaper *The Voice* to complete your study of online, social and participatory media. You could be asked to discuss these products in light of any area of the theoretical framework. There are three types of question in Paper 2. Each one will focus on a different media form studied in depth, and three of the four forms will be assessed. In relation to these CSPs, you may be asked to discuss an issue around audience or industry or context, or, as Paper 2 has a synoptic element, it is possible that you may be asked to discuss the social media accounts using more than one area of the theoretical framework. Questions 2, 3 and 4 on Paper 2 are worth 25 marks each.
- **Please note**: 2024 is the final assessment year for the Zendaya social media CSP. From 2025 it will be replaced with Taylor Swift's social media.

> See Chapters 1 to 7 in the Student Book.

Introduction and context

Zendaya (Zendaya Maree Stoermer Coleman) is an example of modern celebrity. She is a popular US actress and model. She has had some success in the music industry and has been featured on the front covers of many magazines and as a model in advertising campaigns. She makes an interesting case study as she represents the traditional idea of an A-list celebrity who is rewarded for her talents, is part of a high-profile Hollywood couple and represents a modern version of high glamour in many of her public appearances. She also uses social media platforms to engage with her audience and promote her brand identity.

Zendaya's career

Zendaya began her career as a child model and then performer on the Disney Channel. She starred in the sitcom *Shake it Up* from the age of 14 and took the lead role in another sitcom, *K.C. Undercover,* five years later. She also appeared in a number of Disney-produced films.

She began to build a reputation as a glamorous presence at red-carpet premieres and other celebrity photo opportunities, such as awards ceremonies. She tends to wear high-end designer clothing on these occasions, and photographs of her appear in traditional media and on social media. Zendaya appeared in US reality TV as a guest judge on *Project Runway* in 2014 and 2015 and was a runner-up on *Dancing with the Stars*.

She starred in the Spider-Man films *Homecoming* (2017), *Far from Home* (2019) and *No Way Home* (2021) and was celebrated for her portrayal of drug addict Rue in *Euphoria* (2019). The Spider-Man films brought her into the mainstream, introducing her to broader audiences, and her subsequent relationship with the Spider-Man actor Tom Holland increased her tabloid appeal.

▲ Promotion for Disney's *Make Your Mark: Ultimate Playlist*

▲ Zendaya

🔗 **Zendaya's social media accounts:**
- **twitter.com/zendaya (20.8 million followers)**
- **instagram.com/zendaya/?hl=en (185 million followers)**
- **facebook.com/Zendaya (19 million followers)**

While under contract at Disney, Zendaya launched a music career, having hits with her single 'Replay' and a song from the soundtrack of *The Greatest Showman*, 'Rewrite the Stars'. She has written songs that have been sung in *Euphoria*.

Zendaya has also had a very successful modelling career, modelling for many brands including Dolce and Gabbana, Dior and Lancôme. She has written a style book, launched her own shoe brand, a size-inclusive, gender-inclusive clothing brand and has collaborated with designer Tommy Hilfiger on a fashion collection.

Her film and TV performances have given her the opportunity to develop from a child star into a performer of various roles as an adult, and her success has given her a platform to promote a wide range of charities, and political, social and health-related causes.

While she has found success via the traditional media of TV, film and print advertising, social media has helped Zendaya to amplify her fame and she has been able to use it to create and shape her brand identity and her public persona.

Zendaya's social media presence

Currently, Zendaya uses X (formerly Twitter) and Instagram. There is an official Facebook account, but it has not been updated since 2020. Until summer 2023, she had a website at www.zendaya.com. It was then closed down and, at the time of writing, has not been updated or replaced. She also has a YouTube account (4.03 million subscribers), youtube.com/channel/UCKjrT7t9h6GsSkzhFe0ccDA, that largely promotes her musical output although it does contain other promotional material.

■ Star persona / brand identity

Zendaya is known around the world. She has constructed a number of different identities that combine to create her unique star persona.

Zendaya's transition into an adult star has been helped by her film and TV choices. Starring in the Spider-Man films brought her to the attention of a much wider audience in terms of gender and age. Her character MJ was presented as an outsider who, while being very attractive, was admired for her quirkiness and intelligence. *Euphoria* gave her an opportunity to explore darker topics that include addiction, gender and sexual identity, and romantic relationships.

There has also been a focus on creating a brand identity that is associated with high-end, luxury cosmetics and fashion brands, which has associated her star persona with glamour and old-style Hollywood stardom. She has nurtured an identity that is 'normal', approachable and individual while also being glamorous and representing an idealised beauty.

An aspect of Zendaya's star persona comes from her involvement in social issues around gender and ethnicity. She has spoken out against systemic and casual racism and has addressed her position as a role model for younger girls and the power of her fandom. She presents herself as having modern, progressive and inclusive values, and many of the roles she has played reinforce these ideas. MJ in *Spider-Man* is not stereotypically feminine, often wearing gender-neutral clothes and low-key make-up, and rejecting the idea often assumed that women should be sociable and 'likeable'. In *Euphoria*, Rue's sexuality is fluid and undefined. She has a relationship with a trans woman and does not adopt conventional and socially defined labels of gender or sexual identity.

While these characters may be seen as simply roles she has played, they reinforce the idea of Zendaya as a modern woman who is not bound by traditional gender positions and expectations. However, she is also celebrated for her beauty and her thin body. Fashion and advertising images tend to present Zendaya in a more traditional way: she is associated with high-end designer products and is often photographed in styles reminiscent of 'old-Hollywood' where glamour was a marker of idealised femininity.

Audience

■ Target audience – demographics and psychographics

Zendaya's complex star persona means she appeals to a range of different audiences. Initially, she would have appealed to young people, mostly female, while appearing in Disney's young people's programming. She played strong female characters in her two main Disney projects. Rocky in *Shake it Up* is a smart, strong character with a social conscience, and KC Cooper in *K.C. Undercover* is intelligent and capable and, although a high-school student, is part of a US government spy organisation. Success at Disney will help actors to create a fan base, but such popularity can be short-lived as the actors grow out of their roles. Disney is well known for nurturing talent that goes on to wider success, including Ryan Gosling, Justin Timberlake, Britney Spears and, more recently, Miley Cyrus and Selena Gomez. These performers have managed to broaden their appeal to develop longer-lasting adult careers. Many young Disney stars have not been able to do this.

Zendaya's career history might suggest that she is more likely to appeal to female audiences. Her Disney TV shows targeted girls and her roles were positive, active representations of female characters that communicated empowerment messages of self-determination. Her more recent career in modelling has created strong associations with make-up, perfume and fashion brands – associated with older female markets.

However, while Zendaya undoubtedly has feminine appeal, her acting work has made her available to a wide range of audiences and her appeal is broadening as her fame continues. Appearing in niche programmes such as *Euphoria* has positioned her as a brave and versatile actress who is able to represent complex characters in controversial situations. *Euphoria* is often praised for its unique, unconventional visual style. The Spider-Man franchise has more mainstream appeal, with big budgets and high production values. The films use spectacle to entertain and they have also been well received by fans and critics.

■ Audience and media effects

Zendaya was born in 1996 – on the border between millennials and Gen Z – age groups that are often identified as digital natives (Clay Shirky). Both groups grew up using digital media and can relate to Zendaya as a social media celebrity. There is a section of the audience that has grown up with her as a familiar face, engaging with her as a teen performer and now as an adult. This means that some audiences have been exposed to representations of Zendaya over a long period of time (Gerbner). It could be argued that, especially during her Disney career, Zendaya became a part of the socialisation of some audience groups and that she was part of the mainstreaming of certain values and ideals. Her Disney characters focused on the importance of individualism and also engaged with ideas of loyalty, justice and fairness.

See Chapter 6 in the Student Book, on audiences.

△ Selena Gomez–another ex-Disney child star

Audience response

Different audience groups may perceive Zendaya differently depending on their own experiences of her work and their subjective perspectives. A glamorous advert for a high-end brand may be interpreted as intended by succeeders who would associate the brand with prestige and success. Reformers may respond more positively to Zendaya's advocacy of social issues and they may make a negotiated or even an oppositional reading of adverts that focus on wealth and luxury as this could conflict with their own core beliefs.

Zendaya's use of social media offers audiences the ability to engage with her in a more interactive, participatory way. Following a celebrity on social media is a fan activity. It takes the audience member out of the traditionally passive position of simply being a 'receiver' of information into the more active state of engagement. Social media also allows for an apparent two-way communication between the celebrity and their fans. Zendaya's posts on social media receive strong engagement. A post on X thanking fans for their birthday messages in September 2023 was liked by 161,000 people, received over 6,500 retweets, 3,000 comments and was viewed over 5 million times. Zendaya's Instagram account has over 185 million followers.

Many followers of Zendaya are in the equivalent of a fan community and their comments and responses to posts are an act of *prosumer* activity. Their comments become part of the post's content. This content is usually text based, but some followers add gifs, memes and pictures, often representing acts of textual poaching (Jenkins). The communication sharing between fans in the posts is an act that Shirky identifies as characterising the changing nature of modern audiences and the way they relate to media industries and media products. Media audiences today are not only more active, they are also active participants in the creation and promotion of media products.

> **Quick question**
> Identify a number of gratifications offered to audiences by Zendaya's social media accounts.

> See Chapters 1 and 4 in the Student Book for more on print media and media language. Chapter 5 discusses media representations. For more on skills for the non-exam assessment, see Chapter 9.

Media language and representations

When analysing media language in Media Studies, we are usually looking at choices made by professional media producers. When thinking about social media content, we tend to think about the democratisation of production made possible with Web 2.0 where 'ordinary' people now have access to the technologies that allow them to become prosumers.

This can apply to celebrity social media – and often does. Many celebrities upload personal content, giving followers information about their domestic lives. Celebrities often use social media to enhance the parasocial relationships they have with followers, providing 'behind the scenes' access to their lives. It is worth noting, however, that celebrities usually employ staff to manage their social media accounts and take care to construct the 'correct' messages and use images that support the celebrity's public persona.

Instagram

Professional posts

The following posts are from May 2023 and appear together on Zendaya's Instagram grid.

In character in *Dune*
The Instagram image is a thumbnail of a video. The video is a trailer for the film. The shot is a close-up of Zendaya's face in full costume. The film is 'hard sci-fi' and is an adaptation of a highly popular novel. It is directed by Denis Villeneuve, a renowned and respected director. Zendaya's casting in the film

reinforces the idea she is a serious actor who appears in quality productions and its selection for inclusion on her grid feeds into her professional star persona. The close-up shows the characters' intensity and focus. The shot shows Zendaya in a role unlike any others in her career so far, reinforcing her range and versatility as an actress. In this close-up Zendaya appears to be in a military outfit. Her facial expression and costume connote power and action – traits more traditionally associated with masculinity (Van Zoonen) and so, as in her roles in *Spider-Man* and *Euphoria*, she subverts the binary nature of gender roles here (Butler).

Live singing performance

This image is a shot of Zendaya singing on stage. It is one of a collection of images celebrating recent events and achievements in her career. The image has been taken from the audience's perspective, looking up at Zendaya performing. The angle reinforces the position of the Instagram follower as one who observes Zendaya from a distance, and the low angle creates the effect of looking up, idolising and idealising Zendaya from the audience.

Her collaborator, the musical artist Labrinth, can just be seen behind her, but she is depicted as the most important person here. She is wearing her hair loose. Her stage outfit is a pink and red dress over a white vest, with black over-the-knee boots. Although the dress is short, she is not overtly sexualised. The outfit is visually appealing, but also practical. This is a 'look' that could be emulated by fans and is not simply presented for the male gaze (Mulvey). The lighting for this part of the stage show is red, which enhances the action of the live performance and the active nature of Zendaya herself.

Advertising photoshoot

This image is also a still from a video. The video combines a selfie shot by Zendaya and footage from behind the scenes of a photoshoot for the jewellery brand Bulgari. The thumbnail is from the professionally shot video, showing Zendaya in full. She is wearing an off-the-shoulder fishtail dress and an extravagant jewelled necklace. Her hair is smooth and pinned up. She is positioned against a white stone balustrade, with the pale blue sky and water of Venice in the background. The full body shot and the semi-silhouette nature of her dark dress against a light background emphasises an hourglass figure. Her pose exaggerates the curve of her hips. The low-cut dress creates cleavage. Her body shape here appears quite different from the one on stage.

This posture recreates the curvaceous glamour of mid-twentieth-century Hollywood stars such as Marilyn Monroe and Elizabeth Taylor and positions Zendaya alongside these iconic women. Hollywood stars at that time were not expected to be 'like us'; they were actively constructed to be seen as so beautiful and exceptional that they were 'above' us (hence the term stars). Audiences were meant to admire these stars from a distance. While their look and lifestyles may have been aspirational, most audiences knew this was a fantasy beyond their reach.

Zendaya's look in this image emphasises her body and can be read as 'sexy'. She is kept at a distance, however, and her location, clothes and jewellery mean that she too is an idealised fantasy figure rather than a fully sexualised one. She is presented for the male gaze, but her sexuality is not overt. She is presented more as a status symbol. She looks desirable but not 'attainable'.

The video shows her being photographed to promote Bulgari, and this image is one that the brand would want viewers to associate with it. Bulgari is a high-end jeweller and so wants to communicate class, elegance and sophisticated beauty as its brand identity, reinforced by these images of Zendaya.

Media language and representations

The post itself is interesting as a promotional tool. Celebrities associated with brands are usually contracted to use their social media to promote the brands they work for. There is a comment on the post 'Last night was a dream' and a sound clip of Ella Fitzgerald singing 'Dream a Little Dream'. The video begins with one shot clearly taken by Zendaya (perhaps as her contractual obligation to Bulgari) – a mirror selfie that moves into a brief close-up of the necklace she is wearing – and then continues with more professional footage taken at the shoot.

Personal posts

A very different post was uploaded on 1 June 2022 to wish her partner, Tom Holland, a happy birthday. It is an informal selfie and acts as a contrast to the more professional shots on her grid. This photo shows the two actors in a natural setting without make-up and wearing 'regular' clothing. Nonetheless, it is a professional-looking shot. The shallow focus removes any distraction the mise en scène may have created. Tom Holland is positioned in the centre of the frame. His white T-shirt makes him the centre of our attention in this black and white shot. Zendaya's position (to our right), the fact she is not looking directly at the camera and her dark clothing make her the secondary 'object' in the image. The setting and relaxed body language combine to construct the idea that this was an 'off the cuff' moment that defines the relationship as natural and relaxed.

The decision to present the image in black and white brings more than one connotation. Black and white is associated with artistry in photography and film-making. The unusual focus and the natural poses are reminiscent of French New Wave cinema in the 1950s and 1960s. Black and white photography and film is often also associated with 'truth' and 'authenticity', whereas colour has tended to communicate 'artifice'. This post carries levels of meaning in the way it is presented as natural, relaxed, authentic and yet beautiful. It is worth noting that the lighting has been used to illuminate Holland's face and eyes while Zendaya is more softly focused than the rest of the front of the frame. The image is a careful construction that creates a set of ideas rather than just a simple snapshot as it may at first appear.

Zendaya does use Instagram for purposes outside product promotion or personal communication. Famously, she made a statement on Instagram after a TV reporter commented on her Oscar red-carpet photos. Zendaya wore a Vivienne Westwood dress and had her hair in locs for the appearance. A reporter on *E! News* commented that she thought the hairstyle made Zendaya look as if 'she smells of patchouli oil and weed'. Zendaya identified the racism in the comment and posted the following statement that she had made at the Beautycon Festival. She formalised the response by signing off using her last name, distancing herself from her star persona and emphasising both the authenticity and importance of her message (quoted in, for example, teenvogue.com/story/zendaya-beautycon-2018-hollywood):

> *As a black woman, as a light-skinned black woman, it's important that I'm using my privilege, my platform to show you how much beauty there is in the African-American community ... I am Hollywood's, I guess you could say, acceptable version of a black girl and that needs to change.*

In her response, she identifies the marginalisation of African Americans through the exoticisation of their culture (Gilroy). The (white) reporter's comments reflect an idea of otherness based on an aspect of black culture. She recognises the complexity of identity and the 'white privilege' that exists

▲ Zendaya, with her hair in locs, attending the 2015 Academy Awards

in Hollywood. Beauty is often associated with paleness and she recognises that she may be seen as 'acceptable' when darker-skinned women are not. This reflects the intersectional nature of discrimination (bell hooks) as this 'shadeism' or 'colourism' does not impact on men in the same way.

■ X (Twitter)

Zendaya does not post very regularly to her X account. Again, much of the content is promotional material for her professional work and images from photoshoots. Retweets on the account also give her the opportunity to promote causes she feels strongly about or support tweets from other commentators and fans. In 2020, she used Twitter to promote #sayhername in response to the killing of Breonna Taylor, and she was involved in raising awareness for the anniversary of the Tulsa Race Massacre of 1921. She aligned herself with activists by reposting tweets; rarely adding her own comments, but creating an idea of her values and position through association.

Despite being in a relationship with another high-profile actor, Zendaya's social media does not focus on this side of her life very often. Images and videos of the couple tend to focus on their professional roles rather than their relationship. She has retweeted many posts that have wished her happy birthday, including tweets containing photos and image montages of her. Comments tend to be brief, but the retweets increase the circulation and visibility of the original posts, which are chosen for their positive comments about Zendaya. She sometimes posts memes in reply to posts to communicate an emotional response.

Much of Zendaya's X content, however, is promotional material. The profile image at the top of her X homepage at the time of writing is taken from a forthcoming film (*Challengers*, due for release in 2024) and acts as a promotional shot. She posts trailers and images from her work. These focus on her professional persona and, as on Instagram, reinforce her professionalism and accomplishments as well as her glamorous beauty. She often reposts tweets from the magazines she is featured in.

In May 2023, she retweeted a post from *Time* magazine where she featured in Time 100, an annual list of 100 of the most influential people at the time. Zendaya retweeted the image with a simple heart emoji rather than a comment. The original post includes a quote from director Denis Villeneuve, describing Zendaya as a 'creative force', a 'cultural icon' and as having 'authenticity'. These are terms that reflect the brand identity communicated across her social media: her down-to-earth character ('authenticity'), hard work and artistry ('creative force'), and glamour and beauty ('cultural icon').

The image communicates her ethnic identity as her hair is in braids, and she is wearing a designer ball gown that connotes traditional Western glamour and femininity. Her shoulders are bare, drawing attention to the expensive jewellery she wears. She is also wearing a ring, but this is less visible among the ruffles of the dress. The dress and the background are both red, so Zendaya's face and chest act as a contrast, making her the main focus of the photograph. Her body language is strong and upright, and she has been shot from a slightly low angle. The overall effect of these choices is to reinforce Zendaya's power and importance – the point of the Time 100.

Zendaya's social media accounts seem to be focused on presenting a more traditional type of celebrity as a glamorous ideal. Many of her posts are images of fashion and beauty shoots, red-carpet appearances and promotional material for her work. Occasionally, posts are more personal communication.

> **Apply it**
> Select three different Instagram posts by Zendaya and identify how they use media language to create meaning.

> **Quick questions**
> 1. Look through at least ten rows on Zendaya's grid on Instagram. In three words, describe the star persona that is being created.
> 2. Identify how media language is used to create these ideas.

Media language and representations

She uploaded a childhood photo to Instagram on her birthday in 2023 as well as her thoughts on the death of *Euphoria* co-star Angus Conor. In the main, however, she is representing a high ideal of beauty, and the designer brands she often wears are out of the reach of many of her fans.

> See Chapter 7 in the Student Book.

Industry

One approach to the study of industry would be to look at Zendaya as a producer of media content. This approach is taken in the other sections of this chapter and you could identify how the construction of content is also the commodification of Zendaya's star persona.

Her social media is used to promote herself to both audiences and media producers. Her successful creation of a glamorous and sophisticated identity has made her an appealing 'product' for the fashion designers and make-up brands that pay her to be a model or brand ambassador.

When employed on a film or television programme, actors are often required to take part in promoting the project. They will give interviews, go on chat shows and may make personal appearances. They will also post on social media. Some actors' pay is connected to the economic success of the project.

Having popular social media accounts helps to increase the circulation of content and is also an income stream for modern celebrities. A study of Zendaya's social media would show how the commodification of 'Zendaya' is used to generate income and contribute to the success of the work she does. Her use of social media allows audiences to feel a connection and this encourages their positive engagement with and sharing of the content she creates. Zendaya is able to use this outward-facing version of a professional persona and brand identity to market herself to media producers and advertisers to help her remain prominent and develop a number of income streams.

A second approach is to consider the industrial context of the platforms used to create and distribute social media content as in the following case study on Instagram.

■ Industry case study – Instagram

Instagram was initially launched in 2011 as a photo-sharing app. It was an immediate success and had 10 million users at the end of its first year. It was bought by Facebook (now Meta) in 2012 and its user numbers grew again, reaching 1 billion in 2018. The platform has developed over the years to offer different functions to its users and for companies advertising on it. It began to allow video sharing in 2013 and has been encouraging more video content in response to TikTok's popularity with younger users. Instagram stories and live video were launched in 2016, multiple image posts in 2017, and IGTV in 2018.

The platform has altered the way posts are promoted and the way users can search for content. Some of the changes have been welcomed and some not. In 2022, there was a user protest against the emphasis on video content.

Ownership and control (Curran and Seaton)

The buyout of Instagram by Facebook was investigated in the UK and the US to ensure that the deal would not restrict people's use of other apps or sites. The UK Office of Fair Trading and the US Federal Trade Commission both agreed the buyout did not break fair competition regulations.

As Facebook was buying another social media company, this is an example of horizontal integration. Instagram and Facebook offer different experiences for their users and ownership of both helps Meta meet the needs of a wider audience.

Generating an income (Hesmondhalgh)

Instagram is part of the modern cultural industry context. It exists to generate a profit. Its costs are based on providing a service for its users, and its success is wholly dependent on the number of users it has, the amount of time they spend on the platform and their engagement with the platform's content. The company is part of what is called the attention economy. It competes with all other media and non-media ways in which users can spend their time. Instagram wants to attract the users' attention so they can commodify it.

> **Apply it**
> Focusing on a social media platform that you are familiar with, identify the methods used to attract and keep your attention.

Unlike more traditional media industries, Instagram does not make the content that users consume. It provides the platform for other people to distribute the content that they make. Traditional media companies need to pay creators for the content they offer to their audiences. Instagram gets its content for free for as long as its programming and technological infrastructure continues to attract content creators.

Instagram's income is generated by advertising sales. Advertisers pay to have their ads promoted on the platform. Adverts can be still images, but many are videos. Carousel adverts have multiple images and/or videos within a single post. Business accounts can promote their own posts.

Instagram collects users' data and provides detailed information to businesses in terms of the success of their posts, the demographic profile of people who engaged with them and the levels of engagement. This helps businesses create better-targeted and more successful posts, which benefits the businesses as well as Instagram itself. Business users can direct people to sales websites or sell products directly through the app. Companies see buying advertising on Instagram as a good investment as long as the platform is able to distribute adverts to large numbers of potential customers and that many of these customers engage with and respond to the posts.

Instagram can also generate an income for the creators of content through sponsored posts and affiliate links. Advertisers will pay celebrities and influencers to create promotional content and for driving audiences to a product's website. Content creators' payment is usually based on the number of followers they have. Influencers generate audience engagement and activity that allows Instagram to collect more data and sell the information this generates.

Regulation (Livingstone and Lund)

Online content in the UK is regulated by Ofcom and it can take action to apply the Online Safety Act (2023). The act focuses on content that can pose a risk of harm to users or is in itself illegal. The responsibility for the protection of online users lies with the online media service provider. Users can report to Ofcom content that they feel breaches the act and the service provider has not responded appropriately. Ofcom does not investigate individual complaints, but does monitor complaints to assess if service providers are working effectively to protect their users.

Most regulation on social media platforms relies on the application of the community guidelines published by the platforms themselves. Instagram publishes its guidelines and details the rules it requires users to abide by.

> More information on Instagram's guidelines can be found at: help.instagram.com/477434105621119.

For example, nudity in images is not allowed (except in photos of paintings and sculptures). Users are also told they must abide by the law, including issues of decency, gambling, racial hatred and the sale of illegal or regulated merchandise. Users are asked to conduct themselves respectfully and that threats, hate speech and harassment are not allowed. Instagram uses AI to find and remove content that is identified as breaking the guidelines. These and other regulations are also policed by users, who can report inappropriate content or copyright infringements. Instagram can remove posts, suspend accounts and involve the police where this is deemed appropriate.

Instagram has been at the centre of many discussions about the possible effects of social media on its users. As many of its users are teenagers, they are often the focus of these debates. Much of the concern is over the way Instagram presents representations of perfect faces, bodies and lifestyles to young people, including the use of photo editing tools to enhance and 'correct' images. A user's constant comparisons to their own lives and experiences are argued to lead to depression and stress and problems with self-esteem and body image.

Quick questions

1. Identify why Instagram is a good platform for Zendaya to use.
2. How does Zendaya use or subvert the typical conventions of social media platforms to construct her brand identity?

The solitary nature of social media use is sometimes accused of causing feelings of loneliness and isolation. These feelings can be heightened by the fact that a platform like Instagram is ever-present on a user's phone. Use of the app can become compulsive and mirrors addiction, which means that some users can't escape the images, comments and content it provides. It is difficult to determine the accuracy of these claims, as different users have different experiences of the platform and studies offer different ideas about its impact.

CSP 7: The Killing

- **Platform**: broadcast television
- **Form**: television crime drama
- **Product**: *The Killing* (2007) Series 1, Episode 1
- **Targeted elements of the theoretical framework**: In your work on television, you need to explore two named close study media products. If you are studying *The Killing*, you also need to study Episode 1, Season 1 of Channel 4's *No Offence*. Television is identified as an in-depth media form, so the products should be analysed using ideas from all four areas: media language, representation, audience and industry.
- **Assessment information**: Your knowledge of both programmes will be assessed in Paper 2. You could be asked to discuss these products in light of ideas from any area of the theoretical framework. As Paper 2 has a synoptic element, it is possible that you may be asked to discuss *The Killing* and *No Offence* using ideas from more than one area of the theoretical framework. Questions 2, 3 and 4 on Paper 2 are worth 25 marks each.

The Killing is a Danish crime drama initially broadcast in Denmark in 2007 under the title *Forbrydelsen* ('The Crime'). Series 1 follows the investigation into the murder of a teenage girl and focuses on the lead detective, Sarah Lund. The series is a long-form drama and the investigation provides the main narrative arc. *The Killing* is an example of the Nordic noir, or Scandi noir, genre.

The first season of *The Killing* was broadcast in the UK in 2011 on BBC4. It was deemed a success for the niche channel as it attracted around 500,000 viewers for each episode. It was also a critical success and generated a keen and active fan culture. Viewing figures almost doubled when Series 2 was broadcast on the same channel later in 2011, and the programme maintained this audience for Season 3, in November 2012.

The Killing became a global success and was shown in over 100 countries. It won many international awards, including a BAFTA for best international TV programme and International Emmys for best drama series and best actress in 2008. The programme was remade in the US by Fox Television and broadcast by AMC and, later, on Netflix. The US version (2011–2013) relocated the story to Seattle, but retained the basic story of the Danish version, including the lead character, renamed as Sarah Lindel.

Industrial context

■ Production

> See Chapter 7 of the Student Book for a detailed discussion of industry terms and ideas.

DR (the Danish Broadcasting Corporation) is a public service broadcaster financed through the Danish government. Its funding model is similar to the BBC in that the Danish public pay a licence fee. DR is then free at the point of access. DR produces radio and television programmes and can supplement its licence fee income by selling DVDs, electronic downloads and merchandise and through the international sale of its programming.

As DR is funded with a licence fee, its broadcasts do not carry advertising. DR operates under a public service contract. This means that, among other things, DR is required to provide programming that reflects and caters for the various groups within Danish society. DR is required to reflect diversity and variety as well as make its output accessible for everyone. It is obliged to promote Danish cultural output and provide educational material.

The Killing was made in Denmark and broadcast on DR1 in 2007 and its production was funded by DR in collaboration with ZDF Enterprises. ZDF (Zweites Deutsches Fernsehen, 'Second German Television') is a German public service broadcaster. It too is funded by television licence fees, but also generates an income from advertising on its channels.

■ Distribution

The British broadcaster for *The Killing* was BBC4. This is one of the niche audience channels run by the BBC. It offers a different type of programming from the more mainstream BBC1 and 2 channels and caters to different audience interests. BBC4 is characterised by programmes covering the arts and culture. It produces and broadcasts many documentaries on a broad range of subject areas, from music to mathematics. In this way, BBC4 helps the BBC fulfil its remit to provide programming that promotes education and learning. BBC4 also has a history of broadcasting global media, so is active in 'bringing … the world to the UK'. Its focus on programming that is less conventional could also be argued to contribute to the stimulation of 'creativity and cultural excellence', making BBC4 an important part of the BBC's output (bbc.com/bbctrust/governance/tools_we_use/public_purposes.html).

BBC4 is a digital channel that is free to access. Viewers are expected to have paid the UK licence fee, which allows them free access to all BBC output. BBC4 has a programming budget to make, commission and buy content, including programmes from around the world. BBC4 often focuses on programming that is seen to have a high cultural value.

The BBC4 remit states that: 'BBC4's primary role is to reflect a range of UK and international arts, music and culture. It should provide an ambitious range of innovative, high-quality programming that is intellectually and culturally enriching, taking an expert and in-depth approach to a wide range of subjects' (bbc.co.uk/bbctrust/our_work/services/television/service_licences/bbc_four.html).

Primary to its role as a broadcaster is the remit to provide an international perspective. BBC4 has a history of broadcasting non-English-language programmes. Several of its non-English-language shows are European long-form crime dramas. BBC4 is the British broadcaster for critically acclaimed series such as France's *Spiral* and Italy's *Inspector Montalbano*. It purchased the rights to the Swedish production *Wallander* (also remade in English and broadcast on BBC1 between 2008 and 2016), which was a forerunner for other Nordic noir programmes on the channel, including *The Killing*.

The extent of the success of *The Killing* was unexpected. This has encouraged BBC4 to purchase more non-English-language programmes. Since 2016, Channel 4 has also offered a range of international TV programmes as online on-demand box sets under the banner *Walter Presents*, including *Deutschland 83*.

Quick question

In what ways does *The Killing* help BBC4 fulfil its remit?

Audience

The audience for BBC4 is a specialised and niche audience. The programming offered on the channel does not necessarily have appeal to a broad audience, but it would be incorrect to assume that the BBC4 audience fits into a specific demographic.

YouGov offered the following demographics-related information in 2017 about a 'typical' BBC4 audience member:

- Gender: Male
- Age: 55+
- Social grade: ABC1
- Politics: Left
- Monthly spare £: £1,000 or more

Before the advent of multichannel digital television, people often gravitated to one or two channels and watched shows at the time determined by the broadcasting schedule. Technological developments have changed audience behaviours and programmes can now be accessed on multiple platforms and at any time. BBC4 only broadcasts in the evening, but its output is available on iPlayer at any time.

As BBC4 largely offers arts, culture and documentary content, its audiences are those who largely prioritise information and education gratifications and who experience this type of content as entertainment. Some audiences seek out the cerebral pleasures of learning something new and/or having ideas and expectations challenged. Blumler and Katz's uses and gratification theory notes that audiences are 'goal oriented', so audience members for BBC4 will actively seek information and knowledge from the programmes they watch – or at least that is what they are prioritising at the time of choosing to watch a BBC4 programme. They may prioritise more mainstream entertainment pleasures at another time. BBC4 audiences may enjoy the challenge of engaging with less conventional products and this could be seen as another type of cerebral pleasure.

The Killing offers a range of different gratifications, some of which can be linked to its visual presentation, its position within the crime drama genre and the way it uses narrative devices and creates representations. The fact that it was broadcast on BBC4 creates a set of expectations based on an understanding of the channel's brand. The audience would be justified in expecting *The Killing* to offer something new or an unconventional approach to the genre and/or narrative. The audience may expect a requirement to be

See Chapter 6 of the Student Book for a detailed discussion of terms and ideas from audience theory.

▼ Women are a significant group in BBC4's audience

Gender	BBC4 radio (%)	All radio (%)
Male	58.0	48.0
Female	42.0	52.0

▼ Older viewers are the largest group in BBC4's audience, with 77 per cent being over 40 years old

Age	BBC4 radio (%)	All radio (%)
55+	45.9	32.2
40–54	31.5	27.8
25–39	18.4	27.4
18–24	4.2	12.6

active in order to gain the gratifications on offer, so the complexity of the story, the storytelling techniques and the fact that the show is subtitled and needs to be read while being watched will be part of the appeal for audiences who enjoy an active, intellectual engagement with fictional stories.

BBC4 scheduled two episodes of *The Killing* back-to-back each week during its initial screening and this demonstrates that the broadcaster is assuming the audience will enjoy engaging with the drama over an extended period of time. Given the other types of programme on BBC4, *The Killing* was likely to find a receptive fan base within the channel's audience.

Among many other things, the audience members for *The Killing* could be:

- curious BBC4 viewers
- fans of crime drama as a genre
- fans of Nordic noir specifically
- people who are familiar with or curious about Danish or Nordic culture
- those who seek cultural capital by accessing a critically lauded, subtitled series
- people who seek a new and unusual television experience
- Danish speakers.

Each group would access the programme and gain very personalised gratifications as well as the gratifications offered by the show's aesthetics, genre, narrative devices and representations.

■ Audience engagement and interactivity

The interactive nature of e-media may have helped spread the word about *The Killing*. *The Guardian* ran a week-by-week episode summary while the programme was being broadcast on BBC4. These summaries were open for comments, so audience members could gather to share theories and ideas about the case and its potential resolution. A community of fans was soon established with a shared discourse of in-jokes, common grumbles and comments on topics as diverse as Scandinavian decor and Sarah Lund's jumper.

> **Episode recaps published by *The Guardian* can be found at: theguardian.com/tv-and-radio/series/the-killing-episode-by-episode.**
>
> **The finale of Series 1 is discussed here: theguardian.com/tv-and-radio/tvandradioblog/2011/mar/26/the-killing-episodes-19-and-20.**

Guardian readership is likely to overlap significantly with the BBC4 audience and, therefore, *The Killing*. The weekly discussion online and the fact that the show was available on iPlayer for audiences who missed the scheduled broadcasts meant that the programme was able to build its audience before the end of the run. Each week, hundreds of comments were left on the episode recaps and this culminated in nearly 1,000 comments discussing the finale.

The Guardian maximised and benefited from this interest by publishing several related articles, interviews and analyses. Not only did it provide entertaining, interactive articles that created a positive response from audiences, its fan community would also encourage readers to the news site. This activity was also good for the programme, providing free publicity on a regular basis, targeting people who were likely to be interested in the show. So, the show and the newspaper each gained from the cultural capital generated by the other.

■ Audience appeal / gratifications

Crime dramas work on the gratifications created by the enigma of the narrative. Mysteries offer a cerebral appeal for audiences who want to engage with the puzzles in the story. For some audience members, this will mean trying to work out the answers as the story develops, while others will enjoy just watching the investigation unfold. Long-form crime dramas often offer narrative surprises with twists to the plot and in the actions of characters. These surprises can often include the presentation of false heroes (Propp) and the use of red herrings (false clues). The use of restricted narration creates mystery and suspense and the ability to surprise the audience when certain events occur or when information is revealed.

As crime dramas deal in dark and often taboo content, there is an element of voyeurism in the viewing experience. The viewers are shown events that they are not usually able or allowed to see, including, potentially, things that people would actively avoid in their real-world experiences. Episode 1 of *The Killing* offers Nanna's fear and terror and Pernille and Theis's grief and anguish, as well as Sarah and Jan's horror and dismay when Nanna's body is discovered. The characters' emotional journeys provide a vicarious gratification for the audience.

The violence in crime dramas is sometimes problematic. The popularity of the genre means that many audiences are shown many versions of a dark and dangerous world of violence. This could create a view that the world is more dangerous than it actually is (Gerbner's mean world syndrome). Statistically, very few people are impacted by the types of crime depicted in the genre, but many serial killings, child abductions and other violent crimes are shown in TV and film fictions. In addition, news and documentaries often focus on these types of crime. This may culminate in audiences feeling that they happen more often than they do.

It is also suggested that the repeated viewing of violent imagery could desensitise the audience to the real-world consequences of violence. Some crime dramas may do this by disassociating from the victims or by glamourising violence and violent characters. Other crime dramas try to avoid this by humanising and centring the victims so audiences feel the loss of a character, or by dealing with the outcome of the violence by including its effects on family members, investigators or the local community. In *The Killing*, the initial focus on Nanna's emotional state and then on her family encourages the audience to empathise with the terror and grief caused by violent acts rather than enjoy them.

The slow development of the narrative over the series of *The Killing* provides in-depth studies of place, character and motivation that some audiences may appreciate over the fast-paced storytelling offered in episodic shows such as *CSI Vegas*. Long-form drama can tell more complex stories that require audience engagement, which in turn offer gratifications in the intellectual rewards provided by the story. Long-form dramas can also provide excitement by having fast-paced elements within the narrative. *The Killing* combines both elements. The need for exposition in the first episode means it takes its time to introduce the characters and the problems within the story. Later episodes include dramatic scenes that keep the audience engaged with the twists and turns of the narrative as it develops.

The Killing features realistic characters, from Sarah Lund who struggles to balance her professional and domestic roles, to Pernille and Theis, who are loving parents but who make mistakes and react badly when under pressure. Viewers can identify with them and their situations, heightening the emotional connection with the programme. This type of engagement promotes audience loyalty, helps to retain viewers and encourages further audience interaction through social media and so on.

British audiences may be attracted to a drama set in Denmark that offers an insight into Danish culture as well as showing the landscapes and interiors

> **Apply it**
>
> Media products that offer violence to entertain audiences can be very popular. There are many reasons why audiences are drawn to these products. Do you think *The Killing* offers any of the following? If so, where and how?
>
> - The excitement of an adrenaline rush.
> - The ability to see taboo images or engage with taboo ideas.
> - Experience of things that are not part of our everyday lives.
> - Feelings of anxiety or fear – while being in a safe environment.
> - The ability to use our emotional imaginations.
> - Experience of chaos – while being in total control of our environment.

▲ Lund-style jumpers

> **Quick question**
> How does Episode 1 of *The Killing* engage the audience and maintain interest?

of a society that is both similar to and different from their own. The climate reflects the damp, grey winters of the UK but the language and some aspects of Danish culture may feel unusual and even glamorous to the British viewer. Scandinavian style has been used to sell products for many years and British audiences are familiar with IKEA and, more recently, the Danish concept of hygge (encapsulating ideas of being cosy, snug, warm and comforted). Sarah Lund's jumper became iconic, representing hygge as well as being a no-nonsense, practical item of cold-weather clothing. People sought to buy a 'Sarah Lund' jumper and it even had its own website giving a short history of the design, advising where it can be bought and offering knitting patterns for people who wanted to make their own.

Media language

> See Chapter 2 of the Student Book for a detailed discussion on reading audiovisual media, and Chapter 4 for more on media language terms and ideas.

■ Genre

The Killing is an example of a crime drama. Crime drama is one of the most popular and widespread genres in television fiction and in film. It is a genre based on the type of story being told – where the plot centres around a crime of some sort and, usually, the investigation that follows. These are the core elements of crime drama, but the genre can be divided into many different subgenres – each with a different approach in the way the plot is presented. For example:

- Some crime dramas are **hybrids** where the crime plot is presented within the codes and conventions of another genre. Crime dramas can be westerns, science fictions and even comedies. *The Expanse*, shown on the US Syfy network, began as a crime drama set in a future society where space travel is a day-to-day reality.
- **Police procedurals** focus on an investigative team within a specific area of the police force. They are sometimes called cop shows. *CSI* was one of the most successful police procedurals in the 2000s. The original series set in Las Vegas led to three spin-offs (*CSI: Miami*, *CSI: New York* and, more recently, *CSI: Cyber*). *CSI: Vegas* was rebooted in 2021.
- **Single-detective crime dramas** focus on one detective (sometimes a member of the police force, but not always) who appears to have special crime-solving abilities. In *Sherlock*, Holmes is represented as a genius whose personality issues (he has a drug addiction and describes himself as a 'high-functioning sociopath') allow him to see the world in a way that others cannot, thus helping him to find the truth. Not all 'detectives' are detectives. They can be lawyers, authors, journalists or, in the case of Agatha Christie's Miss Marple, observant elderly ladies.
- **Heists** usually provide the audience with the criminal's point of view. Heists tell the story of a crime being planned and implemented. This subgenre often involves a sympathetically represented criminal gang. The Spanish series *Money Heist* is a successful example of this subgenre.

Crime fiction is a long-established and popular literary genre. Many television crime dramas are based on characters and situations taken from successful books. Television programmes featuring popular detectives such as Poirot, Sherlock Holmes, Miss Marple and Father Brown are based on nineteenth- and twentieth-century crime novels. Crime fictions were popular in silent films at the start of the twentieth century and later became a mainstay of television programming. The genre's long-lasting popularity helps to minimise the economic risk for producers.

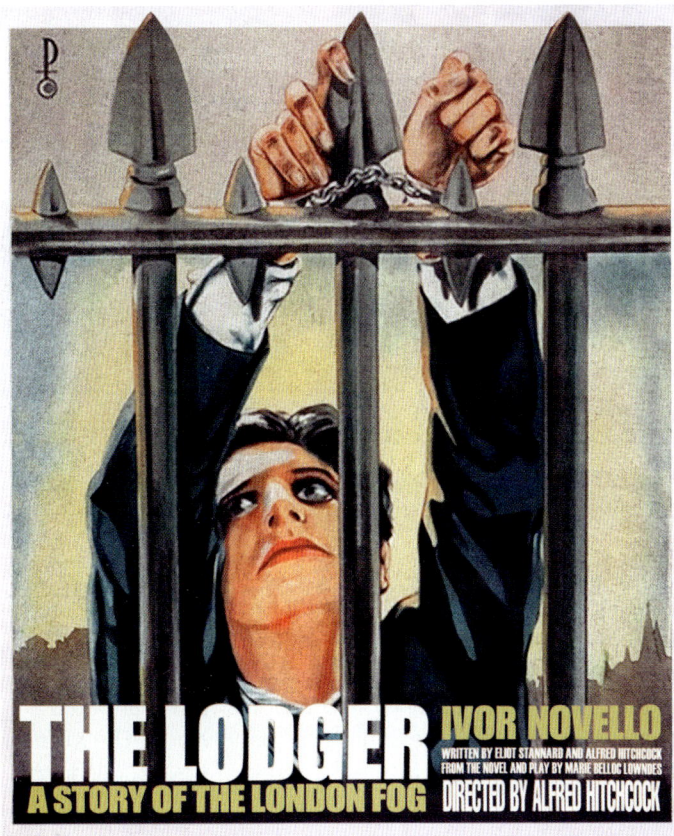

▲ Silent film *The Lodger* (1927, directed by Alfred Hitchcock)

▲ *Dixon of Dock Green* – a popular TV series in the UK from 1955 to 1976

The longevity of the genre shows that it has great audience appeal and its fundamental simplicity means that it can be presented to audiences in many different settings. The genre can be reinvented in many ways and, as long as a crime story is still central, it is possible to give the viewers what they expect from the genre while also offering new and different experiences. In this way the genre can provide familiarity and difference (Neale).

Noir

One subgenre of crime drama is noir. Noir began as a film genre. Film noir ('black film') was the term used by Nino Frank to identify a genre of US crime films of the 1940s that dealt with dark themes, had cynical characters and used a stark visual style. The films were seen to reflect bleaker aspects of US post-war society and the genre often told stories about crime gangs and hard-bitten private investigators, and were often violent. Antagonists were usually arrested or killed, and the protagonists often ended the story alone and isolated, making the genre part of what Thomas Schatz calls the genre of order. Film noir is defined in part by its feeling and tone and the style of its storytelling.

Visually, noir was influenced by German expressionism, a style of film-making that used high contrast between dark and light,shadows and brightness in its aesthetic. Two highly influential German expressionist films are the horror films *Nosferatu* (F.W. Murnau, 1922) and *The Cabinet of Dr Caligari* (Robert Wiene, 1920). These aimed to create feelings of suspense and uncertainty for the audience, using surreal imagery and high-contrast (low-key) lighting to tell their dark stories of death and madness, influencing the style and content of film noir.

Apply it
- Search YouTube for clips from old TV crime dramas. Some popular programmes from the past include:
  - *Dixon of Dock Green* (1955–1976)
  - *The Sweeney* (1975–1978)
  - *The Bill* (1984–2010)
  - *Miss Marple* (1984–1992)
  - *Inspector Morse* (1987–2000)
  - *Agatha Christie's Poirot* (1989–2013).
- In what ways is *The Killing* a typical crime drama?
- How has the crime drama changed over the years?

Media language

△ *The Third Man* (1949, directed by Carol Reed) – a classic Hollywood film noir

△ *The Cabinet of Dr Caligari* – an example of German expressionism

Nordic noir / Scandi noir

The terms Scandi noir and Nordic noir were first used to define a specific style of crime fiction that was being written in the Nordic countries such as Denmark, Iceland, Finland and Sweden. As in other cultures, these countries have a long history of crime fiction and many of the works were translated into English and found an audience in the English-speaking world. *The Killing* was written for television, but it has also inspired a series of novels, taking the genre back to its literary roots.

Nordic noir shares several characteristics with film noir. The stories deal with the darker side of modern life, focusing on violence, crime and their impact. The settings can be both urban and rural, but often focus on the desolate nature of these locations, using isolated areas of the countryside or run-down parts of cities and towns to create a dystopian landscape. The locations and the crimes act as symbols for the wider culture, where the external appearance of families and social institutions hide dark, violent and corrupt behaviour. Scandinavian countries are known for their cold winters with short, dark days, and the climate often influences the presentation of the story. Protagonists in Nordic noir are usually flawed in some way – they may struggle with human interaction or relationships and they often find themselves in conflict with authority figures. The stories often deal with taboo subjects and, unlike typical film noir, feature female protagonists.

■ Narrative

The Killing is a long-form serial drama. Series 1 consists of 20 hour-long episodes that focus on one case – the murder of Nanna Birk Larsen. The series begins with the discovery of the teenager's body and then progresses through a number of enigmas: Who is she? How and why did she die? Who killed her? Each episode represents one day of the investigation. The lead protagonist is a female detective (Sarah Lund) who investigates the crime with her (male) police partner (Jan Meyers).

The series follows a number of storylines that run parallel through the series:

- **The investigation** – The police's progress in trying to solve the crime.
- **The family** – The emotional impact of the murder on the victim's family and their attempt to understand what has happened.

- **Local politics** – A politician (Troels Hartmann) who is campaigning to be Mayor of Copenhagen.
- **The detective's personal life** – The impact of the investigation on Lund's family and relationships.

The connection between the political storyline and the murder develops over the course of the series. The investigation takes the detectives into various locations that represent different areas of Danish society, for example the school and social lives of teenagers. Later in the series, racism and attitudes towards female sexuality are dealt with.

▲ Nanna's parents

Episode 1 offers exposition for the audience and creates the equilibrium for each storyline. The story begins *in medias res* (in the middle of the action), showing a young woman running through a forest in fear for her life. She is shown to be terrified and bloody, and, with the anchorage created by the programme's title and the intercutting of the action with the title sequence, it is clear that this first scene is the main disruption to the narrative. Offering the disruption at the start of the narrative in this way creates immediate enigma as the cause of the events on the screen is not shown. As *The Killing* tells its story slowly, it is important to engage viewers immediately, so they will be prepared to take some time to get to know the characters.

As the whole series deals with just one case, *The Killing* develops gradually, unlike an episodic crime drama where the culprit needs to be revealed within one hour of television. This makes for a slower, more detailed narrative in which characters can be established and then developed. In Episode 1, for example, Nanna's mother Pernille calls her husband, Theis, home to help her deal with a flood in their kitchen. This mundane, domestic scene shows their relationship in a positive way. Pernille teases Theis and they are shown to be comfortable and playful with each other. At this point, the audience knows that their happy life is about to be disrupted and seeing them like this creates pathos, heightening the audience's identification with them when they receive the news about their daughter. This scene also contrasts with the way their relationship will be impacted as they try to deal with the loss of their daughter. Events cause the characters to change and this makes them more complex and realistic.

Media language

In the first episode, we learn that Sarah Lund is about to leave Denmark to marry her boyfriend and make a new life in Sweden with him and her son. We are shown that she is a popular and well-respected detective. We are also introduced to Troels, his campaign team and his political opponent as well as Nanna's best friend at school. The characters are part of separate narrative strands that are drawn together via Nanna's murder.

The whole of Episode 1 is a slow disruption of the equilibria of the various narrative strands within the story. The normal lives of all the characters we are introduced to begin to disintegrate as the episode progresses. This shows the audience that the diverse characters and situations are in some way connected. There is an early connection between the murder of Nanna and the political campaign as the politicians have to cancel a debate because of the investigation – held at Nanna's school. Pernille and Theis's domestic life is about to change for ever and Sarah's domestic plans are postponed as the investigation begins.

The episode ends with the identification of Nanna's body, confirming the audience's assumptions about who the victim is and finalising the various disruptions. The multiple open narrative strands reinforce a state of disequilibrium in all the storylines. Enigma is maintained as the narrative is restricted, so the audience now knows little more than the characters. The closing montage acts as a summary for the various narrative threads. In order to find out the answers to the questions the audience will need to watch the next episode and, ultimately, the whole series.

Apply it
What questions do you have at the end of Episode 1 about …

- the crime
- Sarah
- Sarah's family
- Jan
- Nanna's family
- Nanna's friends
- the politicians and the political campaign?

Media language

Nordic noir has a distinct aesthetic style. The tone is muted and dominated by cool colours such as greys, blues and greens. The colours represent the wintry, often rainy settings, and the limited use of bright and primary tones reinforces the darkness of the genre's content. This limited palette creates an effect similar to the black and white of classic noir and, by using these earthy, natural tones, the shots can use low-key lighting to emphasise the effect of light and shadows. Many of the scenes are set at night, which also offers the same scope for high-contrast lighting. Diegetic lighting comes from lamps, torches and streetlights. By hiding some of the content of the frame, an idea of mystery is maintained as we are unable to get a clear image of what is happening.

Nanna revealed – (1 min 30 secs)

In the opening scene of Episode 1, Nanna is shown largely by moonlight, although we see that there is someone else in the woods who is carrying a powerful torch. As Nanna runs, we are shown glimpses of her, so the final shot of the opening sequence is a shock. In this shot, Nanna is lit by the lights of a plane as it passes above her. This acts as a spotlight and reveals the character as well as her emotional and physical state. The shot only lasts a very short time, so viewers are not able to dwell on this, but are given an opportunity to engage with the character's terror.

Diegetic lighting is also used in interior shots to break up the light and create shadow, reflection and silhouette. In this way, light is used to hide as well as reveal. A shot of Lund in her office shows her in partial shadow and silhouette. The light source is the natural daylight through the window and the reflection of an overhead strip-light. As viewers to this scene, we are positioned outside the office, looking in through the blinds, and our view is obscured by the reflections – the police officers on the left and the strip lights are not in the office with Lund, but are reflections from the room behind the camera.

Sarah in her office (8 min 16 secs)

The cut to mid-shot allows us to see more of Lund's face, but we are still looking at her from outside the office, through the blinds. The camera has pulled in close but we are still being kept at a distance. The bright morning light behind Lund puts her in silhouette and the blinds create shadow.

This series of *The Killing* is set in early November. The exterior scenes use the diffuse nature of winter light to create tone and atmosphere. Here the high-angle shot emphasises the vast and bleak landscape as the police begin their search. The damp ground, the grey sky and the blue tone are evocative and communicate the cold and damp nature of the setting of the story. There is little life in this landscape, which reflects the genre's theme of death and decay.

As each episode represents one day, the lighting changes as time passes. Nanna's body is found as the sun goes down, and the change in tone as the light fades reinforces the desolate nature of the landscape. As night falls, the scenes are lit with police lights, floodlights, torches and headlights. This takes the audience back to the lighting used in the first scene of the episode: Nanna's terror as she tried to escape her attacker has been replaced by her parents' grief when her body is discovered.

Fast-cut editing is used in the opening scene of the episode. The title and credits are intercut between images of Nanna running. The speed of the editing makes it difficult to make out detail, but it communicates the panic and fear being felt by the character. In the main, however, the programme is characterised by a slower editing style. The camera is often static or moves slowly in a pan or a tracking movement to create a sense of space or scale.

Towards the end of the episode, when Sarah joins the search for Nanna, she is presented in ways that encourage the audience to identify with her and her point of view. We are shown what Sarah is looking at. Close-ups and shallow focus shots invite us to identify with her further.

△ **Sarah Lund**

> **Apply it**
>
> Watch Episode 1 of Season 1 of *The Killing*.
>
> - Identify specific media language choices made in the production of this episode.
> - Why have these choices been made? What effect do they have? Complete the table below left.

> **Quick question**
>
> How is media language used to create tone and atmosphere?

> See Chapter 5 of the Student Book for a detailed discussion of terms and ideas from representation theory.

When Sarah is looking for Nanna, the music is quite sparse and consists of some piano notes, a few ambient chords and extended gaps where low-level background noise replaces the soundtrack. The music is used to reinforce the desolate atmosphere created by the mise en scène as well as the action at that moment in the narrative – the search for the missing girl. As the police get closer to and finally discover Nanna's body, the music becomes more ominous, and when Theis is told they have found his daughter, the tension breaks with a mournful theme.

The music that accompanies the montage at the end of the episode communicates tension and a sense of urgency. Rhythmically, it is reminiscent of a heartbeat. Close-ups create an emotional focus that is reinforced by the music.

	Media language observation – where and how	Reason for the choice	Effect of the choice
Camera			
Editing			
Lighting			
Mise en scène			

Representations and contextual issues

The representation of women in *The Killing* includes several characters who have different roles in the story and the narrative:

- **Sarah Lund**: mother, detective, fiancée, protagonist
- **Pernille Birk Larsen**: mother, wife, sister
- **Nanna Birk Larsen**: daughter, friend, teenager, victim
- **Rie Skovgaard**: politician, lover.

Pernille is the mother and wife who begins the story, located in the domestic sphere. She is defined through her relationship with her children and her husband. Rie is shown at first in a purely professional role. She is a political advisor, and it is only later in the episode that it is revealed she is also Troels' lover. The introduction to Sarah shows her in the process of leaving the Copenhagen police force to move to Sweden with her teenage son to marry her Swedish fiancé. It is clear she has status within this professional environment as well as the respect of her colleagues.

There appears to be a male-dominated culture in her team (Sarah is given a sex doll as a joke present), but both Sarah and her colleagues appear comfortable with her place within the group. We are told that she will be working with the Swedish police once she has moved, but it is clear that relocating will mean losing some of her professional standing. At first, she appears to have made choices where her domestic role will be more dominant, but when she begins the investigation, she makes choices that prioritise her professional role over her domestic one. In this way, Sarah reflects the conflicts experienced by many women who have to balance domestic responsibilities with professional positions.

When Sarah is preparing to leave for Sweden, she looks relaxed and feminine. She is shown with her hair loose, wearing jeans and a T-shirt. When she begins the investigation, she ties her hair back and, for the rest of the episode, is shown wearing a Fairisle jumper and an overcoat. Sarah's clothes and the fact that she wears very little make-up allow her to avoid a sexualised gaze. She is an attractive woman, but this is not presented as an important part of her character. The camera presents Sarah in ways that communicate where she is, what she is doing and her thought processes. The audience is encouraged to see her as an accomplished professional rather than judge her on the way she looks.

The representation of Sarah avoids creating a gender-based conflict between her and the men she works with. The gender issues Sarah deals with are based in the realistic tensions created by the needs of both parts of her life. Even in the first episode, it appears that Sarah is more successful in what might traditionally be regarded as the more masculine aspects of her life. Domestically, she has a tense relationship with her son and is distracted by her work when speaking to her fiancé.

■ Context – gender and the crime drama

There have been criticisms of crime dramas and other media products that use violence against women as a narrative device, in that they may:

- naturalise violence against women
- repeat the perception that women are weak and vulnerable
- reinforce the idea that women are victims
- deflect attention away from the violence experienced by males
- offer prurient pleasures showing the brutalisation of women.

There are concerns voiced about the way so many crime dramas are based on the victimisation of women and that the way this violence is represented belittles women. Female victims are often used as devices to allow the story to focus on its main subjects: the detective and the criminal – often male characters. Some US series, such as *True Detective* and *Hannibal*, have used images of anonymous dead women as aesthetic displays. These disposable victims reinforce ideas that women have less value than men – other than to be used and/or looked at. Women's bodies are often on display in the genre, either as murder victims on mortuary tables or where the camera focuses on a woman's injuries. The way the camera often lingers on dead or injured women could be interpreted as being misogynistic – revelling in and fetishising their injured bodies. It is the repetition of these types of image that is argued to desensitise the audience to the violence used to create them.

A counter-argument, however, could be that the use of female victims in these narratives reflects the fact that women are statistically more likely to be the victims of violence. Some crime dramas do attempt to sensitise the audience to the violence to draw attention to the horrifying nature of these acts. Some programmes create more audience identification with victims who are presented as realistic characters. Violence against realistic characters is more likely to shock the audience and create an emotional response that is empathetic with the victim.

In *The Killing*, we are asked to experience the terror of Nanna's final moments in the opening sequence. Although Nanna does not appear again in the main storyline, we are encouraged to see her as a real person through the slow reveal of her back story as the series progresses. The audience is also positioned to see the impact of the murder on her friends and family, showing the broader consequences of the violent act.

Similarly, female detectives can offer an alternative to the 'woman as victim' narrative. Women like Sarah Lund are active and powerful. Although she is a flawed character, she shows that women can act to protect themselves and others. Lund's gender becomes irrelevant as she is a detective first and foremost.

> **Apply it**
> There are many ways to approach representations in *The Killing*. Consider the way the first episode creates and communicates ideas about:
> - the police
> - families
> - teachers
> - politics/politicians
> - Denmark.

The issue of the media's representation of violence against women is complex. Real-world violence affects many women as victims of crime and domestic violence. Media products that engage with this are reflective of a reality where violence against women can come from many different sources.

△ Female detectives in *Jessica Jones* (top) and *Broadchurch* (bottom)

Revelations about sexual abuse started the *#MeToo* movement in 2017, which highlighted the extent of a range of different types of sexually aggressive behaviours experienced by women in many contexts. *The Killing* offers a representation of a female victim who is terrorised, abused and discarded. However, it also offers a range of other women who, in their own ways, show strength and reject the idea of being solely victims. Women in *The Killing* are shown as strong within the home and the workplace, and their feminine characteristics are shown positively rather than being a problem to be overcome, but the programme also acknowledges that violence is also a reality for some women.

> **Quick question**
> How are Sarah Lund's relationships with her job and her family represented in the opening episode?

CSP 8: *Lupin*

- **Platform**: broadcast television
- **Form**: television crime drama
- **Product**: *Lupin* TV series
- **Targeted elements of the theoretical framework**: *Lupin* is a 'full' close study product. This means that you will need to study media language – specifically mise en scène, narrative and genre; media representations; audience; media industries; and the specified wider contexts for this product (social, cultural, economic and political).
- **Assessment information**: In the exam, you will be comparing Series 1, Episode 1 of *Lupin* with Series 1, Episode 1 of *The Responder*, a UK-produced police drama first broadcast on BBC1 in 2022. You will be required to respond in essay form to a 25-mark question based on the two programmes. You may be asked about any part of the theoretical framework you have studied or the wider contexts of the programmes.

Lupin (Netflix, 2021) is a French crime thriller television series inspired by the short stories and novels about Arsène Lupin, Gentleman Burglar by Maurice Leblanc.

Media language

■ Mise en scène and characterisation through costume

Mise en scène in *Lupin* is frequently cinematic. Paris is generally signified as a genteel place, an attractive and clean city with cafés, bridges, picturesque streets and historic buildings with distinctive rooftops. This is in keeping with common romanticised semiotic productions across cultural products in representing Paris. We see a slightly different side to the city when Assane visits Vincent's flat. The tower blocks of the suburbs are signified as uniformly grey and oppressive in comparison with the wealthier and older parts of the city.

The necklace that is the object of the heist narrative supposedly having belonged to Marie Antionette is an iconic symbol of the monarchy prior to what is now the French Republic. A necklace belonging to Marie Antoinette was also at the heart of a pre-revolution scandal involving a courtier and conwoman in an event that is well-documented in French history. In this episode, it connotes the historical end of an era of social inequality and the founding of the French Republic's values of liberty, equality and fraternity. The necklace is significant because the exposure of contemporary social inequalities and those caused by racial discrimination are at the heart of *Lupin*.

Selecting key stills from different scenes can allow a greater understanding of how images within key scenes function semiotically to convey meaning. Some examples follow, but you could choose your own.

- The dress code of Assane's grey boiler suit and hat signify his anonymity and ability to pass himself off as an ordinary person.
- The reflection of the necklace foreshadows its doubling up later, and the existence of a copy.

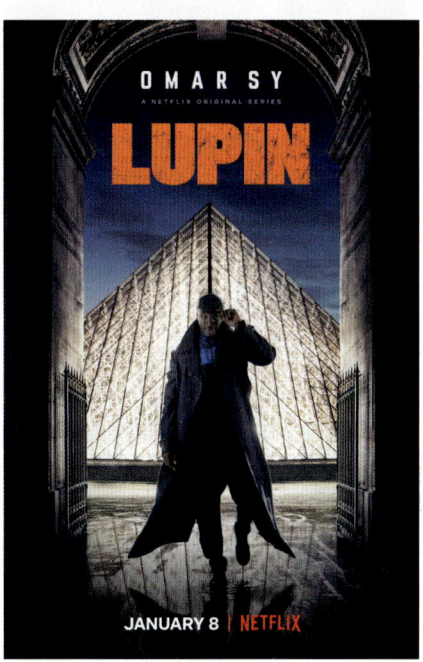

▲ Advert for Series 1 of *Lupin – In the Shadow of Arsène*

> **Apply it**
>
> The examples here have looked at how to decode mise en scène. Now choose a short scene from the episode.
>
> Analyse it using the following technical codes of audiovisual media:
>
> - camera movements
> - editing techniques
> - audio codes.

🔗 **For more on decoding audiovisual media, see Chapter 2 of the Student Book.**

- Selective focus on Assane shows his gaze and focus to be fixed reverently on the necklace, signifying his desire for it.
- Assane's dress code is smart but casual, particularly his shoes – his clothing is otherwise unremarkable, affording him invisibility when he wants it.
- Claire is in a Parisian-chic trench coat and boots with tailored trousers – she looks more professional.
- The proxemics between the two connote a relationship in this two-shot, but non-verbal codes and communication reveal Claire leaning backwards slightly and Assane towards her, signifying tension.
- Assane's dress code here in a purple suit looks regal and signifies wealth and confidence. Unlike most others there he doesn't wear a tie, connoting a dislike of rules and convention.
- The sycophantic clapping of the wealthy Parisians as he arrives and the positioning of Assane versus the other attendees at the auction signify the power structures at work in French society.
- Low lighting sets the scene for subterfuge at the Louvre.

Narrative

Narrative techniques in the opening episode

Lupin uses a serialised narrative form. The plot involving the heist apparently completes and is therefore 'enclosed', and there is also satisfactory narrative closure provided by the scene with Assane, Raoul and Claire towards the end. The narrative also integrates a number of flashbacks, which gradually reveal the story behind Assane's association with the Pellegrini family.

A cliffhanger is presented in the form of police officer Youssef's discovery of the link between Lupin and his alter-ego Sertine. There are other hermeneutic codes that the viewer assumes will be developed as the series progresses, such as the whereabouts of the necklace until its recent rediscovery, and whether his father, Babakar Diop, was involved in its original disappearance.

Development of a heist narrative

Heist narratives are distinctive because they often ask us to empathise with the criminal. For Assane, his participation in the heist is warranted by his motive in wanting to reconnect with his son and avenge his father.

Heist narratives are more commonly associated with films, and the adaptation of this heist to television is indicative of the borrowing of contemporary television drama from cinema in terms of production values, stars and even budgets.

Conventional heist narratives feature several stages:

- Recruitment of a specialist team by the mastermind behind the heist where each has a role. In this case, Assane is the mastermind, Kevin is 'the muscle', Vincent is 'quick and decisive', and car thief Rudy is the driver.
- Planning: This is mainly explained in the sequence in the loan shark's flat, where Assane describes what will happen.
- Enactment of the heist, in such a way that the audience can take pleasure in seeing it unfold while being aware of what is going well and what is not.
- Aftermath: Here, this also involves the capture of the loan shark and retrieval of the necklace by police, only to discover it is a fake. Flashbacks show us a second, more complex heist plot was being enacted by Lupin in anticipation of being double-crossed.

Applying narrative theories to the episode

Roland Barthes' five narrative codes are a useful tool when considering the serialised nature of this narrative as the first instalment of the series. The following table gives some examples of these.

▼ Barthes' five narrative codes

Hermeneutic codes	<ul><li>What is driving Assane to steal the necklace?</li><li>Will he repair his relationship will Claire and Raoul?</li><li>Will Youssef discover his real identity?</li></ul>
Proairetic codes	<ul><li>Kevin holds Assane over the balcony, then pulls him back into the flat.</li><li>Rudy loses control of the car; it crashes through the roof of the gallery.</li></ul>
Semic codes	<ul><li>Assane's varying dress code signifies his ability to blend into any environment.</li><li>His apartment décor connotes refinement and education.</li></ul>
Symbolic codes	<ul><li>The injustice done to Assane's father and his plot to avenge it.</li><li>His desire to normalise family relationships and repair the family unit.</li></ul>
Cultural/ referential codes	<ul><li>The Louvre as location.</li><li>The *Mona Lisa* painting.</li><li>The book about Lupin given to Assane's father and then to him.</li></ul>

Todorov's theory can be applied to the main elements of the heist plot:

1 **Equilibrium** – Assane Diop works as a cleaner in the Louvre. He has a strained relationship with his ex-partner and their son.
2 **Disruption** – Assane visits a loan shark who threatens to throw him off the balcony of his apartment because he has not brought the money he owes.
3 **Recognition** – The loan shark and his henchmen realise Assane is much more than he appears when he easily fends off a second attack.
4 **Attempt to repair** – The heist plot: the loan shark and his associates agree to help Assane while planning to keep the necklace for themselves.
5 **New equilibrium** – The men are caught. Assane uses his guile to keep the necklace. His relationship with his former partner and their son begins to improve.

Other ways of applying the theory might be to consider the plot of the backstory, the disappearance of the original necklace and the blaming of Assane's father for the crime, or focus on the subplot of his desire to improve his relationship with his ex-partner and son.

Applying Levi Strauss' binary oppositions reveals a range of tensions that drive the narrative. For example:

- **Wealth v poverty**: There are numerous ways in which this is explored. Consider the snobbery and institutionalised racism of the Paris elite versus the world of the loan shark; the refinement and poise of Assane, his apparent natural charm and intelligence that, it is implied, come from self-education rather than privilege (Assane begins with nothing as the son of an immigrant who worked as a driver/domestic help, but has built himself a comfortable lifestyle – it appears – by exploiting their world materially).
- **The rule of law v natural justice**: It is implied that Mme Pellegrini is a more sympathetic character than her husband, but she fails to defend Babakar – it is left to Assane to avenge his suicide by making the necklace disappear for a second time.

Apply it
Can you find any other examples of binary oppositions in the narrative? Try to identify two more and give a full explanation of how they operate in the episode.

For more on learning to apply narrative theories, see Chapter 1 in the Student Book. Structuralism and Levi Strauss are covered in Chapter 4.

Postmodernism – intertextuality and the Lupin novels

Adaptation can be interpreted as a form of intertextuality. This is particularly the case when the source material is significantly altered to play with the ideas in the original. *Lupin* changes the race of the lead character and engages with ideas relating to fandoms in popular culture by making one of the investigating officers a fan of the series. So, the series refers to a world outside itself. The show has led to a rejuvenation of interest in the Lupin short stories and novels.

Genre

Lupin is a hybrid genre, drawing on a range of generic influences from television and cinema (some examples are in the following table). The blurring of generic influences in this way is a strategy by the producers to reinforce the appeal of the programme, combining elements from multiple successful formulas and traditions. Some of these subgenres could also be considered story types or even 'master plots'.

One reason these formulas are so successful is because they are timeless, with many having predecessors in classical theatre or earlier decades of film and television.

▼ Some genres and forms that have been combined in *Lupin*

Crime caper/heist	Although there is typically a lot of overlap between these, crime capers tend to be less gritty than heist films. They also feature charming and charismatic protagonists and may have some lighter-hearted, even comic, moments and characters.
Con	Con films or television programmes often feature a complex anti-hero who is able to skilfully deceive others. Much of the pleasure is in the plot and second-guessing motives and actions.
Drama	These often use flashbacks, backstories and emotive storylines – personal conflicts and struggles, often relating to social issues.
Crime drama	Crime investigation drives the plot, often by an unconventional investigator.
Revenge thriller	A wrong done to the protagonist sees them pursuing someone to mete out justice – complex and fast-paced plots.

Genre theory and *Lupin*

Lupin most strongly correlates with genres of order (Schatz) as it incorporates characteristics of male-driven genres such as the revenge drama and heist film. It centres on the social class and race-influenced power struggle between Lupin and the Pellegrini family.

Steve Neale suggests that the patterning of genres serves the needs of both audience and industry, giving us a text that draws strongly on a wide repertoire of elements from different but related subgenres and genres. The naming of the series after the character at the centre of it will have an intertextual relay function in transmitting expectations to audiences who are familiar with the original stories. The trailer for the series aroused audience expectations of a charming protagonist against the background of the Louvre as setting, but this may be somewhat arbitrary for audiences not familiar with the original character.

Generic hybridity may also have a role in drawing in an audience that would not usually watch a foreign drama. Familiarity with a range of the genre codes in the trailer makes engagement more likely.

Lastly, the programme engages us with both regimes of verisimilitude:

- The **cultural regime** means we relate to the issues of social class and race and the Parisian location as glamorous – all these factors can be used as connection points for the audience between programme and real world.
- For the **generic regime**, French audiences will comfortably acknowledge Assane's behaviours as in keeping with their expectations of Lupin. For audiences elsewhere, their knowledge of the range of generic codes it selects from make the text comfortable viewing even without this specialist cultural knowledge.

Apply it

By mentioning specific moments in the episode, explore how and why *Lupin* could be considered a generic hybrid.

🔗 For more on genre theories by Neale and Schatz, see Chapter 2 of the Student Book.

Quick questions

1. What four key words could be used to summarise the progression of a heist plot?
2. Write a sentence giving an example of repetition and variation of the mystery/crime genre demonstrated by *Lupin*.
3. Give an example of how dress code can signify meanings about character in mise en scène.

Representations

Key areas to explore in *Lupin* include gender and race, immigration, the family and representations of place. We have already considered how a predominantly romanticised view of Paris is constructed through mise en scène. The iconography of Assane's Paris is so conventional and aesthetically pleasing that the Paris Tourist Office promotes the filming locations from the series as a feature on its website. Expansive, wide-angle and high-angle shots of the city and its streets represent it favourably. These coincide with the expectations many people will have of Paris, based on previously encountered representations in film and television.

■ Race and postcolonialism

It is possible to study representations of race in *Lupin* using postcolonial theory. Senegal was only freed from French colonial rule in 1960, and, even today, Senegalese education is conducted primarily in French, despite many of the population not speaking it as their first language. The legacy of colonialism can be seen in the migration of Assane and his father to France as part of the contemporary African diaspora, where many Senegalese then found the only jobs available were low-paid positions.

Many members of the African diaspora would be able to relate to the double consciousness experienced by Assane, who is very aware of how he is seen by the rich white people he and others from migrant communities work for. His father experiences routine micro-aggressions and casual racism, such as not initially being recognised by Mme Pellegrini. Assane experiences similar when Juliette invites him to swim to her for a kiss. For a black audience, there is cultural syncretism and universality to the experiences of the Diop family.

Family is another interesting area to explore. Assane's mixed-race family is one that many modern families can relate to. It is a family with separated parents, but it functions, and everyone within it has the will for it to work. Near the beginning of the episode, Claire refuses the child support money offered to her by Assane, showing that she values his relationship with their son over any financial contribution. He in turn plants the money in her pocket without her noticing, which she then accepts. In the final scene, the relationship between Claire, Assane and Raoul is presented as harmonious and tension has been resolved.

■ Assane Diop – stereotype or countertype?

Assane signifies a countertype of Frenchmen. For one thing, the character of Lupin from 1905 would have been seen or assumed as white, so, to choose a black actor for the role signifies a more modern and inclusive representation of the character.

The programme-makers have encoded some of the issues experienced by black Europeans through narrative context and dialogue. Assane's assertion that no one 'sees' him because he is black and therefore part of an out-group articulates the stereotype of the immigrant doing low-paid, invisible work at the Louvre. This is exploited by the character as a source of power and control over the in-group and a source of narrative pleasure for the audience. The idea that the only way he can better himself is through crime, however, is more stereotypical.

In terms of masculinity, we can consider Butler's approach. Assane conforms to the trope of the heteronormative 'gentleman thief'. His character motivation is represented as loyal to his own intrinsic values, which conform to cultural expectations of masculinity. These include physical strength and the ability to fight. He is 'honourable' because he seeks to avenge his father. Father-and-son relationships are performed as a part of his masculinity. The passing on of the book from father to son in each case connotes that the nurturing role of the male parent is limited to promoting a criminal career.

None of these representations is innovative or challenges patriarchy, and repetition of their performances as stylised acts helps to reinforce them as cultural norms.

■ *Lupin* – a version of reality (Stuart Hall)

Lupin offers us a fictionalised portrayal of a confidence trickster and thief living in Paris. But the Paris he inhabits is only a 'version' of reality. Heavy stereotyping is used in the representation of the elite classes at the top of the social pyramid, but it is also present in the representation of the loan sharks in its criminal underbelly.

These stereotypes form a cultural shorthand that allow us to quickly distinguish between 'good' and 'bad' characters as well as to reflect on a range of real-world social issues. Meanings decoded by the audience can be expected to have some degree of polysemy. This could be due to a range of factors such as experience of French culture, the city of Paris, race and social class and even expectations derived from reading the original Lupin books.

■ Applying feminist theories to *Lupin*

There are few female characters in the narrative of Episode 1. A few pointers for applying feminist theories to these characters are given in the table below.

Character	Description/role	bell hooks	Liesbet van Zoonen
Claire Laurent	Long-suffering ex-partner of Assane.	• These white women are secondary characters, in the case of the Pellegrinis from backgrounds that are very privileged. • Black women are therefore marginalised by their absence. • White male privilege is represented by the guests at the auction and M. Pellegrini in particular.	• Gender imbalance in the significance of roles played by men and women. • Female characters are subordinate to males in most respects and only appear in secondary roles. • Women are wives, ex-partners or femmes fatales (distortion).
Anne Pellegrini	Although kind to Babakar initially, she fails to defend him when accused of the theft.		
Juliet Pellegrini	In flashback as a teen temptress (a common trope), but also a danger or threat to Assane. Later represented as hugely privileged inheritor of the Pellegrini estate.		

Quick questions
- Make one argument that Assane is a stereotype, and another that supports him being a countertype.
- Give one factor that could affect how an individual viewer decodes the meanings in *Lupin*.
- Which real-world organisation uses the series to promote itself?

Industries

■ Production, distribution and circulation

In 2018, the European Parliament responded to concerns from European television industries about cultural imperialism and streaming services by introducing a quota rule for streaming services. Under this rule, services such as Netflix must carry at least 30 per cent content that originates in the region. In addition, the rules require that platforms financially support the development of indigenous media by investing in the production of local content directly or by contributing to national subsidies.

Gaumont, commissioned by Netflix to produce the *Lupin* series, is the oldest film company in the world. This demonstrates Netflix's willingness to collaborate with experienced regional and domestic media producers for quality content with a transnational appeal to satisfy more than just the regional market.

VoD services such as Netflix have a great deal of financial power in the market to commission other production companies. These programmes are, however, subject to cancellation at short notice if not performing as expected. Although Netflix is not transparent about ratings, these flexible business practices serve its interests well. At the time of writing, *Lupin* has three series, suggesting it is performing sufficiently well.

■ Media regulation and on-demand television

Netflix is not, at time of writing, regulated by Ofcom. The UK government has, however, produced a draft media bill that intends to bring it under Ofcom's authority. An extract from the impact assessment of the bill offers reasons for the need to change legislation (assets.publishing.service.gov.uk/government/uploads/system/uploads/attachment_data/file/1166204/VoD_Regulation_Final_IA_-_PLS_publication_version.pdf):

- UK viewing habits have changed with the growth in VoD.
- VoD is not robustly regulated, if at all, in the UK.
- Many VoD services are based outside the UK and so do not have the same standards they would if regulated by Ofcom.
- Any changes in regulation need to target bigger producers specifically to balance freedom of expression against protection from harmful content.

This shows the conundrum at the heart of all decisions about media regulation as explored by Lunt and Livingstone – that media regulators must strike a balance between protecting consumer rights to make free choices about what to watch and protecting vulnerable viewers from potentially disturbing content. There is also a contradiction in that free-to-air, satellite and cable services are regulated internally, but the viewing habits of some audiences may be bypassing this altogether, rendering it meaningless.

Maturity ratings are currently set by Netflix to determine the suitability of programmes. In the UK, this takes the form of the familiar age certifications used by the BBFC. In the case of *Lupin*, the series is rated 15 for themes of suicide, depiction of violence and discrimination. Parental controls can also be used to prevent the accidental or unsupervised viewing of inappropriate material.

■ Hesmondhalgh and the cultural industries

Lupin is a truly internationalised pop cultural product, and a result of a globalised media market that considers stars as well as genres and narratives to be readily saleable commodities. These strategies mean almost guaranteed audience success. The risk taken on by Netflix in producing *Lupin* has thus in some ways been minimised.

David Hesmondhalgh observed that the apparent choice and freedoms we have in consuming cultural products brought to us by digital technologies and web use is largely an illusion, given that the ownership of these industries is so concentrated. The dominance of Netflix on the VoD sector seems to confirm this.

> **Quick questions**
> - Which theorists can you use to support your discussion of the regulation of VoD?
> - What is unique about Gaumont compared with other production companies worldwide?
> - What proportion of content has to be originally produced in Europe according to the rules of the 'Netflix quota'?

Audiences

In the first three months of streaming, *Lupin* attracted over 76 million viewers worldwide and was Netflix's most watched series at the time, as well as one of its biggest debut series.

Different audience interpretations are possible, and these may be accessed by applying reception theory or by a developed study of the wider contexts of the programme, which engages the audience in part through its treatment of contemporary social issues.

> **For more about reception theory see Chapter 6 of the Student Book.**

■ From domestic television to transnational phenomenon

Changes in broadcast technologies have had a far-reaching effect on how audiences encounter television products. Today, the ability to access a huge variety of programmes has also allowed many audience members to broaden their tastes, with foreign dramas (which were once seen as niche products for a middle-class audience) being a good example. These can be summed up as in the following table.

Broadcast era	Post-broadcast era
Scheduled television on individual channels	TV players, streaming, VoD
Limited choice of content	Vast choice of content
Domestic market and production – smaller budget and lower production values in serial drama	Globalised production – larger budgets, high production values
Stars are more commonly seen in television or film rather than both	Stars may appear in film and television
Watched on television sets	Watched on a range of devices
Freeview/'terrestrial' television	Paid subscriptions, cable and satellite, online
Content produced for non-English speaking countries has little opportunity to reach others	Widescale dubbing, subtitling and distribution of foreign television outside country of origin

Omar Sy was already a popular and well-loved actor in France, so *Lupin* would always have attracted a good audience there, at least for Episode 1. Of more interest to us is the way in which a drama can appeal so broadly beyond national boundaries in the era of transnational media distribution.

Neale's genre theory tells us that audiences are seekers of novelty as well as lovers of predictability, and Netflix's highly productive business model of producing a high volume of original products as well as being their key distributor means it can spread and absorb risk better than, for example, some smaller film studios. There are aspects of *Lupin*, however, that appeal beyond the cultural specificity of the source material that inspired the series. The heist narrative, the charisma of the lead, the high production values and well-developed secondary characters, as well as the setting in a city which has global renown, all contribute to its appeal.

How media producers target, attract and potentially construct audiences

The largest share of Netflix's audience demographically is aged 18 to 34, with slightly more women than men having accounts in 2023 (52 per cent), with the average annual salary of subscribers being lower than £40,000.

Much of the construction of audiences by Netflix is through trailers and targeted marketing on its own platform. Watching any similar generic content, or even just heavy promotion at launch point, means that potential viewers see trailers of a programme on their home screen or featured as tailored suggestions based on past viewing.

Word of mouth and social media often play a role as well. Audiences often publicise what they are currently watching to friends online as well as in real-world conversations. Trailers on YouTube are a large part of Netflix's strategy. Interviews with stars, chat show appearances and cross-media promotion such as magazine interviews also play a role.

In the case of a high-value series, there is other official content. There are behind-the-scenes videos designed to feed fandoms. The basing of the series on such well-loved sourced material also makes fandoms more likely to evolve. *Lupin* writer George Kay suggests that programme-makers now actively welcome and encourage fandom as part of their strategy to reach audiences: 'A lot of our favourite shows have their own podcasts and fanbase and all of that stuff, and I thought it'd be cool if that was incorporated into the series itself, so it becomes like an adaptation "live" within the series' (radiotimes.com/tv/drama/lupin-french-sherlock-holmes).

Applying audience theories to *Lupin*

Cultivation theory

For media effects, we must look beyond the most obvious or predictable claims of social learning theory. It is unlikely that someone would decide to plan a heist based on what they saw on the show. Neither is it particularly likely to cause an outbreak of concern that national treasures are at risk from complex, intelligent thieves seeking vengeance for past wrongs.

Beneath the surface though, there are subtle indicators of certain ideologies and world views being potentially reinforced: what we might think of as socialisation through the media. These are also an important cultivation effect.

Uses and gratifications

The series as a whole fulfils a diversion gratification, since *Lupin*'s narrative is immersive and its heist narrative far removed from the everyday. Personal identity might be experienced in seeing Assane's intelligence and charisma as qualities to admire, and social relationships have often been a key gratification producers aim for – that people want to share their experience of the programme with others. This is particularly true of streaming services where a whole series may be binged in a short period of time, increasing its immersive and shareable experience.

Surveillance could also be fulfilled in experiencing another culture's products and being aware of what is new on Netflix. Following trends is an important gratification for many, and some audience members will have been brought to the show out of curiosity from seeing it 'hyped' online.

> **Apply it**
> Discuss the following as possible examples the audience might find of resonance, enculturation or socialisation through the media:
> - People with the greatest wealth in European cities are predominantly white, exploitative and view themselves as superior to other people.
> - Experiences of racism are an everyday occurrence for black men in France and this has not improved for many decades.
> - Only low-paid jobs are available to people from migrant communities.
> - Crime offers an escape route from poverty.

> **Quick questions**
> - In which age range are the biggest subscribers to Netflix?
> - Name two key differences between the broadcast and post-broadcast eras of television.
> - Which use or gratification do you personally feel is most fulfilled by this first episode?

Audiences

The wider contexts of *Lupin*

■ Cultural context

Although not well known in the UK, Leblanc's novels occupy a similar cultural niche in France to Conan Doyle's Sherlock Holmes stories, which were also written in the early 1900s. Also significant is the role of the Louvre gallery as a location and the featuring of the *Mona Lisa*, both iconic signs of France's tradition of high culture and art.

France has a long tradition of crime, thriller and mystery series. Particularly popular in France are television police procedurals and a tradition of French film genre, *films policiers*, which are crime thrillers featuring an embattled protagonist, influenced by Hollywood film noir.

■ Social context

The series explores issues relating to social class and race in contemporary France. Although nine-tenths of its population are French-born, Paris is home to many immigrants and their descendants from former French colonies, particularly in North Africa. Protagonist Assane and his father are originally from Senegal. Over 60,000 people who were born in Senegal were recorded as living in the greater Paris region in the 2019 census (insee.fr/fr/statistiques/6455264?sommaire=6455286&geo=REG-11#ancre-IMG1B_V2_ENS), making a postcolonial reading of representations in the episode very useful. The racism experienced by Assane and his father at the hands of the Pellegrini family is repeated in the present day. Job insecurity and the necessity of taking low-wage jobs just to make ends meet also features as a subtext in the lives of Assane and his father.

■ Economic context

Key to discussion of the economic context of *Lupin* is an understanding of the role of Netflix in contributing to the continued survival of television drama in the post-broadcast era. This is in part due to heavy investment in drama series with high production values and commitments to multi-series production to satisfy an audience of binge-watchers. Television dramas now often feature stars who move between television and film as well as having a cinematic production aesthetic.

■ Political context

Concerns about racism in French society are reflected in many French media products and are indicative of a very polarised political scene in France. In the 2022 presidential elections, Marine Le Pen of the far-right National Rally party won 42 per cent of the vote.

Further reading

- *Radio Times* interview with Lupin writer George Kay: radiotimes.com/tv/drama/lupin-french-sherlock-holmes.
- One of a range of official behind the scenes videos made by Netflix and available on Youtube: youtube.com/watch?v=I5TZeyADMWU.
- Interview with director and star in *The Guardian*: theguardian.com/tv-and-radio/2021/jan/27/lupin-omar-sy-louis-leterrier-netflix.
- Draft UK government media bill: assets.publishing.service.gov.uk/government/uploads/system/uploads/attachment_data/file/1166204/VoD_Regulation_Final_IA_-_PLS_publication_version.pdf.
- Fan wiki collating interesting videos, images and so on that are useful for analysis and research: netflix.fandom.com/wiki/Lupin.

Quick questions
1. Which English-language stories are often compared with the Lupin books in terms of appeal?
2. What two main issues relating to social inequality are explored in the episode?
3. Name a related film or television genre that is popular in France.

CSP 9 *GQ*

- **Platform**: print
- **Form**: magazine. Magazines are identified as an in-depth media form, so the products should be analysed using ideas from all four areas of the theoretical framework – media language, representation, audience and industry.
- **Product**: *GQ*, March 2022: the front cover and internal pages provided by the exam board
- **Assessment information**: You could be asked to discuss *GQ* in Paper 2. There are three types of question in this paper. Each one will focus on a different media form studied in depth. So, three of the four forms will be assessed on the paper each year. You could be asked to discuss *GQ* in light of any area of the theoretical framework, such as an audience or industry context, or, as Paper 2 has a synoptic element, you may be asked to discuss it using more than one area of the framework. You will also need to explore *The Gentlewoman* to complete your study of magazines. Questions 2, 3 and 4 on Paper 2 are worth 25 marks each.

> See Chapter 11 of the Student Book.

Industry

GQ (*Gentlemen's Quarterly*) is an established lifestyle magazine for men. It offers entertainment and information content on a broad range of fashion, style and culture topics, including sport, technology, music and travel. Its content defines a lifestyle for its target audiences and reflects their interests, hobbies and pastimes.

> There is more on the magazine industry in Chapter 7 of the Student Book.

GQ was first published in 1931 under the title *Apparel Arts* and was an industry publication for wholesale and retail clothing businesses. *Apparel Arts* was passed on from clothing businesses to their customers and became very popular, leading to the launch of *Esquire* magazine in 1933, which offered varied content for the general public as well as a focus on clothing.

Meanwhile, *Apparel Arts* continued to be published and became *Gentlemen's Quarterly* in 1958. As the name suggests, it was published four times a year and was now aimed at consumers rather than businesses. It was rebranded as *GQ* in 1967 and became a monthly in 1970. The title was bought by Condé Nast – a multinational conglomerate owned by Advance Publications, which has business interests in (among others) Reddit and Warner Bros Discovery – in 1979. *Esquire* was acquired by the global publisher Hearst in 1986 and the two magazines have become competitors.

Advertising, marketing, promotion

Many modern consumer magazines have similar 'catalogue' origins and provide a similar function. Modern magazines inform readers of products and services that they may want to integrate into their lifestyle. The media form is, therefore, a vehicle for the makers of consumer products to raise awareness of and persuade readers to desire and (hopefully) purchase what they are selling.

Contemporary magazines traditionally have two main income streams. They charge readers for the product and advertisers for page space. Advertising costs are based on the size of the advert and its position.

> **Apply it**
>
> Look through a paper copy of any magazine:
>
> - Work out the rough percentage of the pages that contain adverts.
> - Look for content that is promotional in nature. Work out the rough percentage of pages that contain promotional material.
> - How do these percentages compare to the total amount of non-promotional information and entertainment content offered by the magazine?

> 🔗 **You can access more corporate information on Condé Nast at: condenast.com.** The website provides an insight into the range of media produced by the company including its global brands. You can see how it markets itself to potential advertisers at: **condenast.com/advertising**.

Magazines often generate further income by producing promotional material within their content. Deals will be made with producers of consumer goods to promote their products in a variety of ways. Fashion photoshoots, make-up tutorials, competitions and buying guides are all methods of promotion. An interview with an actor, for example, promotes the TV series or films they are appearing in.

Magazines are commodities that need to appeal to an audience to be successful. The nature of magazines is that their profitability is also linked to being useful to other companies as a promotional tool.

■ Condé Nast

Condé Nast is part of the cultural industry and is a global media conglomerate. The company is based in the US, but creates media content for audiences around the world. Condé Nast was founded as a magazine publisher in 1909. Its first title was *Vogue,* an upmarket fashion magazine. It now publishes a range of titles for different audiences including *Wired*, *Bon Appétit*, *Condé Nast Traveller* and *Vanity Fair*.

Over the years, Condé Nast has expanded by merging with or acquiring other media companies. It has taken over magazine publishers (horizontal integration), allowing it to expand its portfolio of titles and reduce competition for audiences in some areas. *Wired* was acquired in 1998 and offered a new audience for the company. It has also diversified by buying into online content (such as Reddit and Pitchfork), gaining access to new audiences and new technologies.

This diversification of output in recent years responds to changes in technology and audience behaviours and expectations. Print magazines, with their reliance on hard copy sales and advertising revenue, have seen profits decrease as audiences move online. Magazines are expensive to print, relatively bulky and their content is fixed until the next issue is published. In contrast, online media is often free, more accessible, more portable, more up to date and provides almost infinite variety. An immediate response to this in the magazine industry was to provide audiences with a website. Publishers now recognise that social media engagement is an important factor in being economically viable as it has created new income streams that help to replace the loss of income in the print industry.

Condé Nast has diversified across its range of titles. For example, the cookery magazine *Bon Appétit* has a successful YouTube channel providing a range of food-related content including 'how to' videos and looks behind the scenes at restaurants.

■ *GQ* across media platforms

GQ uses online and social media to support and promote its brand. Its YouTube channel offers videos that are often based around celebrity questions and answers (Q & As). It has a highly successful series where actors 'break down' characters they have played (youtube.com/watch?v=hkO8qXCFYWA&ab_channel=GQ).

GQ has multiple Instagram accounts – many based on the different international editions of the magazine, such as britishgq. This account publishes images and quotes to encourage audiences back to its website and/or the magazine itself. It also promotes '*GQ* Recommends', a newsletter that sends information on 'products, deals & launches' to its subscribers.

The website offers a subscription to the print magazine and its digital edition as well as providing content including sections on fashion, watches, culture and grooming. The website includes video content and a shopping guide. There is also a section called 'GQ Heroes', a feature relating to an annual live event (which is also streamed). The event and the web content focus on wider social and cultural issues, including racism, gender issues, as well as 'heroes' from sport and culture.

Innovating by using social media and offering digital issues of the magazine aims to keep *GQ* relevant, keep audiences interested and meet these audiences' ever-changing needs and expectations.

GQ promotes itself as a successful brand with 1.8 million followers on social media and a 7.3 million global reach (*GQ Media Kit,* 2022). The global readership of *GQ* in 2019 was 934,000 (nytimes.com/2019/11/02/style/mens-magazines.html) compared with the magazine's circulation of 1.3 million in 1995 (nytimes.com/1995/05/08/business/the-media-business-with-2-awards-under-its-belt-gq-is-more-than-a-clotheshorse.html).

> **Quick question**
> Explain why *GQ* is no longer simply a print magazine.

> The *GQ Media Kit* is available at: **cnda.condenast.co.uk/static/mediapack/gq_media_pack_latest.pdf**. The kit is aimed at advertisers, meaning that it offers lots of information about audience, content, brand identity and advertising rates.

Audience

■ Target audience

We continue to look at the ways the magazine addresses the audience and attempts to create appeal in later sections on media language and representations.

> Theories mentioned here are defined and discussed in Chapter 6 in the Student Book.

Demographics

The target audience for *GQ* is young adult males who largely fall into ABC1 socio-economic categories. The target age range is identified as 20 to 44, making this a magazine for men who are in the early to mid-stage of their careers. There is an assumption that readers would be relatively economically secure, making them a valid audience for the advertisers in the magazine.

Psychographics

While age, gender and economic status are useful ways to think about the audience, there may be many who fall outside these groups. For example, having interests in technology, sport and masculine fashion is not necessarily dependent on gender. Given the fluid nature of gender identity, it would be more accurate to define the audience as people with interests in the kind of content offered by the magazine. Not having the finances to be able to buy into the more luxury brands featured in the magazine may not necessarily exclude a person from enjoying the publication. A reader may have aspirations towards the lifestyle on offer or may simply be interested in looking at something different from their day-to-day experience.

■ Reception theory (Stuart Hall)

The way a media product is interpreted cannot be fully controlled by the publication. Its media language choices attempt to fix meaning and promote the producer's intended meanings, but individual readers will make their own interpretations, which may not always coincide with the intent. Individual interpretations can depend on the reader's own *subjective* point of view and may be affected by their personal experiences and circumstances.

Apply it

How might different factors impact the interpretation of the content of the magazine?

Consider the *intended meaning* and how the subjective position of the audience may lead to a *negotiated* and/or *oppositional* interpretation.

An example is given here. You might have other ways to think about the front cover.

Magazine content	Intended meaning	Interpretation based on age	Interpretation based on gender	Interpretation based on ideological beliefs
Punk imagery on front cover	Fun juxtaposition of cultural reference connoting rebellion with Robert Pattinson's star persona as teen heart-throb	Certain audiences may not recognise the cultural references (punk, *Twilight*)		Conservative thinkers may feel shock or distaste if punk is perceived as anti-social and anti-authoritarian

■ Audience gratifications

The magazine offers a range of gratifications for the audience. According to Blumler and Katz, an audience accesses media products to gain specific types of gratification identified as: entertainment, information, identification and social interaction.

Apply it

■ Look through the CSP pages and *GQ* online and show where the following gratifications are offered. Be specific – how does the magazine or online content create the gratification?

Gratification	Where and how?
Entertainment	
Information	
Identification	
Social interaction	

■ Do you think you can add to Blumler and Katz's categories? What other gratifications are available here?

Other gratifications?	Where and how?
Star recognition	The use of Robert Pattinson on the front cover
Aspiration	

■ Summarise the type of person/personality you think would enjoy the magazine. Consider Young and Rubicam's categories to help.

Quick questions

1. Focus on each coverline on the front of *GQ* and identify the gratifications being offered by the magazine.
2. What do the coverlines tell us about the expectations of *GQ* held by the magazine's audience?

Media language

In order to be able to discuss the magazine CSPs, you need a detailed knowledge of the way media language is used in the construction of the pages you have been asked to study. You should be prepared to identify and analyse:

> See Chapters 1 and 4 in the Student Book for more on print media and media language.
>
> See Chapter 8 in the Student Book for more on skills.

Images	Lexis	Layout and design
Composition	Language choices	Typography
Lighting	Headings	Page design
Framing	Mode of address	Headings
Colour		Columns
Focus		Legibility features
Mise en scène		Positioning of images and text

■ Genre

Identifying the genre and the magazine's use of genres codes and conventions is a useful way to begin your analysis:

- The codes and conventions of the form (magazine: front cover and feature article).
- The codes and conventions of the magazine's genre.

Codes and conventions of the magazine form

Conventionally, magazines:

- are print productions
- are published on a regular schedule
- use good quality paper and binding
- feature recognisable elements such as:
  - front cover
  - contents pages
  - feature articles
  - advertising
  - interviews
  - shopping guides.

The front cover

Front covers tend to follow typical visual codes and conventions adapted to meet the needs of the specific publication and its audience. The cover is important as it acts as an advert for the magazine and aims to attract the reader to the issue. The cover is often used to help reinforce the brand identity of the magazine too.

Features you might expect on a front cover include:

- **masthead**: the magazine's title or logo
- **main image**: usually takes up the whole cover with other design elements around it
- **secondary image**: smaller images related to content in the magazine
- **coverlines**: brief descriptions of the content
- **main coverline**: usually bigger than all the others and related to the main image
- **barcode**: pricing information for shops
- **dateline**: date of publication
- **website link**: to direct the reader online.

> **Apply it**
> - In what ways is the front cover of *GQ* conventional?
> - How does it use the codes and conventions in ways that:
>   - relate to the target audience
>   - communicate *GQ*'s brand identity?

Feature articles

Magazines will often use an aspect of their house style in the design of feature articles to ensure there is a consistency of appearance across the magazine. The design of a feature article will always aim for legibility and readability. The feature needs to look appealing to draw the reader in.

Some general codes and conventions of feature articles are:

- a combination of text and images
- a grid design page layout, presenting text (body text) in columns
- headline – the main title of the feature
- kicker – text above the title
- pull quote or block quote – text from the feature displayed as a design feature
- boxes – for images or block quotes
- image captions.

Genre codes and conventions

GQ's genre can be defined in a number of ways:

- **Men's** magazine – contains content that is assumed to be appealing for males. It has a masculine point of view.
- **Fashion** magazine – content mostly focused on men's fashion. Fashion shoots, style guides, use of artistic photography, idealised models. Sophisticated design in the colour palette, page layout and so on.
- **Lifestyle/culture** magazine – while fashion is its main focus, it offers content on other topics related to a specific aspirational lifestyle. Buyers' guides, features on film, music, sport and so on.

The CSP pages demonstrate the need for media products to be reliable and recognisable. Audiences respond to the familiar (Neale) and have genre expectations that need to be met. Magazines retain the style, look and content that audiences have grown to expect while also trying to offer something different each issue in the hope of striking a balance between the familiar and the new that will retain audience interests.

Semiotic analysis

The application of semiotic ideas can help move into more in-depth analysis. For example:

> The front cover of the magazine features a portrait of Robert Pattinson. The paradigmatic choices made in the presentation of Pattinson include very specific make-up and costume choices. His hair has been bleached and styled in a way that creates connotations of the punk movement of the late 1970s. Punk acts as a symbol of rebellion and is often used as a signifier of anti-establishment ideologies. The anchorage created by the blonde hair, white vest and heavy chain are icons that refer to well-known punk figures including Sid Vicious from the Sex Pistols and Billy Idol. Readers would need a specific cultural knowledge to recognise these references, but punk codes are often repeated and the reader should be able to interpret the symbolic meaning without the knowledge of specific musicians.
>
> Pattinson is made up to look as if he has been in a fight. The denotation of wounds on his face reinforces the connotations of anti-establishment attitudes and anti-social behaviour often associated with punk. Given the context of this image on the cover of a high-end fashion magazine and the actor who was a teen-heartthrob early in his career, these juxtapositions could be interpreted as creating a parody of punk rather than a serious communication of punk 'values'.

■ Narrative

Narrative is usually associated with moving-image analysis where information is provided over time and a story structure (beginning, middle and end) can easily be identified. The pages from *GQ* can be analysed using narrative theory. For example, the coverlines position the audience to go on a *quest*. They pose questions and suggest that answers may be found in the magazine. The reader will learn what the '50 Holy Grails of Modern Menswear' are (a grail being a feature in a traditional quest), what Francis Ford Coppola is up to now and the answer to 'Who is Robert Pattinson?' In this way, the reader is positioned as the *hero* and the content of the magazine provides the logic and cause and effect that lead to the problems' answers.

The subject of the feature article, Jonathan Bailey, is initially positioned as facing a problem (he 'felt lost'). His professional role is seen to present a challenge he needs to overcome as the hero of this tale that begins with this sense of *disequilibrium*. His heroic role is reinforced with the focus on his strengths and talent (his awards and 'prolific spell on West End stages'). The scale of his 'problem' grows (*Bridgerton* was 'massive', watched by '82 million households'). His past (told in flashback) offers the *equilibrium* of the story. He came from a tiny village and began building his performance skills early. Having to deal with hiding his queer identity was an initial *complication*. The *resolution* shows how he overcame this based on the *binary opposition* created between his true self and society's expectations. The resolution details his achievement as a successful actor who is able to be 'true to himself' – this is his new equilibrium.

The front cover of the magazine positions the reader as a participant in a story (they need to buy the magazine to take part of course), whereas the internal feature article frames the reader as an observer of someone else's story.

Representations and context

Given the target audience and the images in *GQ*, a key area of representation is gender, specifically masculinity. There are, however, other representation topics that can be discussed.

■ Representations and social/economic context

Representations of young (30s), wealthy, white men tend to dominate GQ. Older men are sometimes featured if they are identified as aspirational role models for the target audience that reflect the brand identity of the magazine. Similarly, successful men of different ethnicities are featured from sport, acting and music.

The common factor across ethnicity and age is the economic status of the men featured. The brand identity of the magazine, with its focus on sophisticated style, means that representations will focus on symbols of success. The magazine uses luxury watches as a signifier of success, and fashion shoots use expensive designer clothes. This representation reinforces the way a materialistic culture defines and recognises success. The focus on expensive consumer goods constructs an idea of the elite lifestyles that the wealthy have access to. For some readers, this will be unattainable, so the representations create a fantasy and escapism from economic reality. Wealthier readers who align with the magazine's values could identify with the signifiers of success and choose to purchase them to communicate their personal identity and their own success. Different audience members respond differently to such representations (Hall).

△ The punk look, London, 1979

Quick question

Break down the media language choices made in the presentation of Robert Pattinson on the front cover of *GQ*.

Identify the reasons for and/or the connotations of the choices made.

Media language choice	Reason for choice	Connotations

See Chapter 5 in the **Student Book** for more on media representations.

The focus on representations of luxury, wealth and success reinforces the values of a capitalist, neo-liberal culture. The magazine promotes the notion of individual success and the idea that status comes from the ability to buy into luxury products and brands. Men from lower economic groups are simply not represented or acknowledged in the world created by the magazine. This idea of class also connects to a specific idea of masculinity that is communicated through the magazine.

■ Representations of masculinity in context

GQ offers a very modern version of masculine identity that in many ways subverts traditional ideas. In the past, masculine identity was often linked to a man's work identity. Men were expected to be strong (especially physically), stoic and have stamina. These qualities were required when undertaking manual work, which was, for many years, associated with manliness. It could be argued that this helped to normalise the hard and often dangerous conditions that men worked in. It identified a range of qualities that were seen to be 'natural' and, therefore, expected in a man. Traditionally, men were not supposed to be interested in the way they looked. Instead, their identity was based on their role as the breadwinner and head of the family, and their strength was seen as a function of their engagement with 'honest' work.

Gender identity was traditionally seen as one side of a binary. Being a man was defined in opposition to being a boy. 'Men' were defined by their rejection of childish behaviours and attitudes. Masculinity was in opposition to femininity, so the definitions of masculinity tended to be qualities that were 'not feminine'.

These concepts of masculine identity have been changing for a long time, and *GQ* represents a range of modern ideas of masculinity that can be seen to reflect societal changes in the expectations of men and the lifestyles they lead. Contemporary ideas of gender identity have begun to challenge some of these conventional expectations and this is evident in the representations in *GQ*.

An interest in fashion would have been seen as 'feminine'. This convention is challenged in *GQ* where ideas around the importance of grooming and masculine fashion and style is communicated throughout the magazine.

The feature article on actor Jonathan Bailey reflects several ideas of modern masculinity. The images that accompany the article are fashion shoots of the actor in high-end fashion. Each photo has a caption that details the designer and the price of each item of clothing. The suppliers of the clothing are recognisable names who have cultural capital. The clothes have been chosen to represent contemporary fashion and style. Bailey has been carefully presented in these images. His hair has been styled and he wears some subtle make-up.

Bailey's facial expressions are 'moody', as he does not smile in any of the images. In two of the images, he is looking into the distance. In the other two, he adopts a direct gaze that is assertive and confident. He makes no attempt to smile and present a 'welcoming' image to draw the reader in. This reinforces ideas of masculinity as strong and individualistic.

Giving the images a more contemporary twist, the clothes Bailey wears are breaking the binary of traditional gender expectations. Some of his clothes (the suit and the leather coat) have connotations of masculinity, whereas others (the blouse-like shirt and the lace-knit jumper) create a softer image in their references to women's/feminine clothing.

△ The full-page, mid-shot image of Jonathan Bailey in *GQ* could be seen to be making a passing reference to James Dean – an actor who represented traditional masculine ideals in the 1950s

CSP 9 GQ

The images are a good example of the breakdown of the binary between the masculine and the feminine, and the accompanying article focuses on the fact that Bailey is gay. The feature shows how gender is constructed and can be seen as being a *performance* (Butler). Bailey is represented as a man who has agency and has taken control of his life. His looks are important, but the feature focuses heavily on his accomplishments, which Van Zoonen identifies as being typical in representations of men. Bailey's sexuality is defined outside heteronormative conventions and he is a successful role model for the male readership. He is presented as an idealised masculine figure who is handsome and well-groomed, but at the same time presents ideas of both masculinity and femininity in his clothing.

The feature indicates that his sexuality was not too much of a barrier to his success, and that his own personal happiness improved once he came out. This reflects changes that have occurred in British culture and reduces the 'difference' often perceived in people who are not heterosexual. bell hooks identifies the impact of the intersectionality of gender, ethnicity, class and sexuality and the way it impacts on individuals. Bailey is queer, but is also male, white, comes from a middle-class background and is now economically successful. His experiences will have been affected by the combination of privileges and discriminations that come with his specific identity.

All of these aspects of the representation of Bailey come from being presented via the male gaze. Laura Mulvey focused on the presentation of women in film but her identification that the camera shows a masculine perspective and frames images through male desires can be applied here. The audience for *GQ* is predominantly male and representations are created for them by writers, photographers and editors who work from within a patriarchal culture and institutions.

The male gaze here is focused on a man, so reflects the qualities men are likely to admire. Rather than the overt sexualisation of women that Mulvey observed, men are often admired by other men for their success and power – in Bailey's case, from his professional role as an actor. As discussed before, success is signified by external objects, such as clothes, and a general idea of a sophisticated style. The images used in this article fulfil this aspect of the aspirational male gaze. While the images are not explicitly sexual, his acknowledged sexual identity and the slightly sultry nature of his demeanour could be interpreted as creating a homoerotic sex appeal.

Apply it

Identify two quotes from the Jonathan Bailey article that create ideas about masculine and/or queer identity. Use the context of the article to explain the meanings they create.

Quick questions

- How can *GQ* be seen to be attempting to minimise its economic risk and maximise profit (Hesmondhalgh)?
- Identify examples of the use of equilibrium, disequilibrium and the creation of a new equilibrium in the CSP pages.
- In what ways is the idea of the fluidity of identity (Gauntlett) present in the pages?

CSP 10 Horizon Forbidden West

- **Platform:** computer games
- **Form:** video game
- **Product:** *Horizon Forbidden West*, a popular action-adventure, third-person RPG (role-playing game)
- **Targeted elements of the theoretical framework**: In the exam, computer games are an in-depth CSP, meaning you will study all areas – media language (including narrative and genre), representations, audience and industries. You are also required to study the cultural context only of the game.
- **Assessment information**: Paper 2 requires you to respond to a 25-mark question in which you will compare the game with popular mobile game *Sims FreePlay*. The similarities and differences between the two games offer an excellent starting point for displaying your knowledge. Studying the mise en scène of the game will be our entry into the game here and allow you to make important links.

Horizon Forbidden West is the second main game following the successful reception of *Horizon New Dawn*. Both games have also had expansions added. A third game is due to be released at the time of writing. Initially the game was only available on PS5, with a Windows version released later.

Media language

Mise en scène and semiotics

The cut-scene that opens the game foregrounds the hyperreal aesthetic of the game world, with wide-angle shots and numerous repeated shots of the character Aloy travelling through it accompanied by her voiceover. This opening establishes a full range of codes that are significant to game-players. The genre is strongly signified through both action and setting; narrative codes are introduced; and the aesthetic of the game is showcased.

🔗 **You can watch the opening of the game at:** youtube.com/watch?v=-j32t0ael0E.

Tribesman against a storm-ravaged landscape background, 0:49

- Sky and background appear sepia toned, an indexical sign of pollution or lack of health in the climate system – an unnatural-looking storm brews above the head of the hapless tribesman.
- Tribesman in the foreground has a minimal dress code, with a simple hand tool and hessian sack for harvesting – these lack the complexity and protective qualities of Aloy's attire and equipment.
- Non-verbal codes connote toil and loss of hope.

Aloy with robotic beast against autumnal backdrop, 1:06

- The red colour of many of the plants and foliage signify autumn, a time of dying back, but they appear lush and vigorous with unnatural growth.
- Aloy appears well dressed for her mission, carrying a range of equipment that connotes her capabilities, with a dress code of protection.
- Her dominance over one of the robotic beasts we have seen running over the plains in aerial shot connotes her power and authority.

Aloy gazes at ruins through the rain, 1:34

- The bleak sky and washed-out tones of the location together with the rain strongly signify narrative problems and challenges and form a juxtaposition with the lush green foliage.
- Selective focus of the scene and over-the-shoulder shot encourage us to share Aloy's view, despite the third-person perspective.
- The overgrown ruined structures are an indexical sign of the post-apocalyptic genre.

> For more on analysing mise en scène, see Chapter 2 of the Student Book.

Apply it

Watch some sections of game walkthroughs, for example on YouTube. From these, select between 6 and 12 screenshots.

Analyse the mise en scène of each using some of the following:

- the framework of semiotics, including orders of signification and types of sign
- codes present in the semiotics, such as dress code, colour codes and non-verbal codes
- use of props, locations and decor
- proxemics (which may be player-driven in encounters) and para-proxemics – where the audience is positioned in relation to the characters
- 'camera' angle, range of player-controlled movements and shot types.

Aim to write about three bullet points for each frame.

■ Narrative

Adventure and enigma and audience participation in constructing narrative

Horizon Forbidden West has a serial quality to the narrative, picking up where the first instalment ended with the first main quest, 'Reaching for the Stars'. The quest narrative form is observed throughout. Hermeneutic codes drive these, with each action and reaction to it driving the plot through proairetic codes.

> For more on Barthes' five narrative codes, see Chapter 2 of the Student Book.

The narrative itself is complex and involves 17 main quests, 29 side quests and 20 errands, which the player can use to build experience points and gain weapons, outfits or armour and skill points. Side quests also contribute to the narrative, enriching it with additional details, characters and experience of new locations. To complete the game and experience the ending, the final quest, 'Singularity', must be completed.

Media language

Feedback on fan forums for the game has sometimes focused on the quality of the narrative disappointing players. For example, the storyline involving the Zenith is singled out by some players as disrupting their immersion in the game's narrative, so that they fail to suspend disbelief.

Fantasy and hyperrealism in narrative

The text as a whole can be read as hyperreal, with a blurring of the distinction between the material world in the present and the game map and vibrant graphics that are used to reconstruct its future. The saturated colours and crisp but detailed graphics contribute to this, representing to us fantasy beasts and objects using the same aesthetic as the 'real'.

Todorov's narrative stages

Todorov's theory is interesting to apply to game narratives, where there are potentially several different routes to what is between two equilibriums. The first equilibrium is usually established through use of cut-scenes, and this is the case with *Horizon Forbidden West*. Reaching the narrative goal of the game, the new equilibrium, is the focus of the majority of gameplay as well as the additional pleasure and narrative context gained from individual quests.

▼ Todorov's narrative stages as applied to *Horizon Forbidden West*

Equilibrium	Aloy is searching for the back-up to GAIA, the AI that can reboot the planet's biosphere.
Disruption and recognition	• Aloy sees the continued damage being done by a terraforming system out of control, such as robotic creatures consuming the environment. • Her search takes her, with companion Varl, to the West and two warring tribes. • Aloy is interrupted in her quest to retrieve the system by unfriendly and technologically advanced humans, the Zeniths, who also take a back-up of GAIA from its hiding place.
Attempt to repair	• Aloy attempts to recover GAIA's sub-systems and get the program to communicate with the others. • The remainder of the game consists of narrative problems concerning: 　• the progress of the civil war between the two tribes 　• attempts to defeat the Zeniths, who are themselves fleeing a technological experiment that destroyed their colony and sent an extinction signal to Earth 　• attempts to retrieve all the sub-systems needed to reactivate GAIA.
New equilibrium	GAIA is reactivated, but Nemesis remains a threat, paving the way for a new game to follow in the series.

Binary oppositions and conflicts

Exploring the binary oppositions that the game presents us with is useful for a game of open-world and exploration elements and where progress may not have the same linearity each play. The open-world structure allows for different quests to be explored, but all of these contribute to the same thematic content.

Narrative ideas are structured around:

- Civilised versus uncivilised. The tribes encountered by GAIA are represented as uncivilised and warlike. They are needed by Aloy and her companions, mainly for their resources or mastery of machines.
- Technology as threat versus technology as potential saviour. The Zeniths are represented as a race of technologically advanced humans; super-rich inhabitants of Earth who used their wealth and technologies to extend their lifespans and flee disaster. This negative portrayal is contrasted with the potential of the GAIA system to restart Earth and prevent ecological disaster.

Cover art

Analysing the cover artwork allows us to put together all of the above, and to understand how it promotes a narrative image for the game. You can view an image of the *Horizon Forbidden West* cover here: http://tinyurl.com/mrk2z5ek.

- Aloy positioned as the centre of visual interest
- Confident, powerful stance
- Hair long and feminine; red hair connotes fiery personality
- Dress code influenced by the traditional dress of Native American tribes – connotes that the 'West' is once more 'wild' and in need of 'civilising'
- The Golden Gate Bridge is a man-made structure, but covered in exotic foliage, signifying post-apocalyptic genre and locating the scene in San Francisco (drawing on generic regime of verisimilitude)
- Water is rough, signifying turbulent times, but colour is clear and blue – unpolluted
- Red of plants and hair – Aloy in harmony with environment
- Robotic pterosaur – signifies futuristic but also primitive or prehistoric state, technology as aggressor
- Lexical coding of tagline, 'Rise above our ruin' – mode of address draws player into game as well as signifying ownership or even collective responsibility
- Invitation to *join* Aloy; *frontier* strongly embedded in US ideologies about exploration, gaining new territories, colonialist values
- Geometric patterning signifies technology of gameplay, open-world nature of game
- Dark foliage but also flowering, 'conceals' potential threat
- *Discover* – exploration
- *Fight* – conflicts – lexical coding signifies mode of gameplay
- *Uncover secrets* – creates hermeneutic codes
- Creates a narrative image for the game of post-apocalyptic action/adventure
- Arbitrary sign of PS5 branding
- Secondary images on back cover show Aloy in medium close-up (MCU), allowing viewer to familiarise with the character
- Secondary images signify gameplay as exciting and conflict-filled

■ Genre

Computer games not only have their own discrete genres but also demonstrate use of familiar genre codes from other media forms. To make the picture even more complex, the narrative image of games in their marketing and the way this is transmitted by word of mouth is also interconnected with modes of gameplay and game mechanics, which are a significant part of the consumption experience.

Genre conventions, action-adventure and the influence of Hollywood

Genre and game mechanics are inseparable in computer games. Games with quite different generic influences from other pop cultural products in narrative, theme, iconography and so on often share the same game mechanics. This leads to some unique hybridisation of modes of play with other, more familiar genre signifiers, such as iconography or character types.

▼ **Modes of gameplay that contribute to genre in *Horizon Forbidden West***

Third person	This is significant for players. The third-person perspective allows gamers to identify with the character while simultaneously experiencing distance from their actions.
Action role playing	The tradition of female third-party action RPGs was firmly established by the *Tomb Raider* series.
Open world	Open-world games feature exploration and finding a route that is player-led and discovery-based as opposed to linear or more structured.
Single player	Single-player games may not appeal to all audiences if the multiplayer experience and competing or collaborating with and communicating with other players is a primary pleasure. It is worth noting here that the multiplayer gaming environment is not always comfortable for female players due to player behaviours, so they may prefer a single-player game.

🔗 **For more on hybridisation of genres, see Chapter 2 in the Student Book.**

Action, adventure, post-apocalyptic and even sci-fi conventions are hybridised in the game, showing clear influences in iconography, narrative and world-building from other media forms. The influence of high-concept cinematic genres that are effects driven is very strong – consider, for example, the *Avatar* films.

The AI narrative draws more on science fiction, but the encounters with tribes, wild and dangerous creatures and an exotic environment are influenced by action adventure, which often features locations that are extreme in some way and sparsely populated. The post-apocalyptic narrative context, with iconography of a post-disaster world where nature has reasserted itself and an 'empty Earth' scenario are also explored, as it is a narrative of survival.

Genre theory

In terms of Schatz and the genre of order, despite the female protagonist, *Horizon Forbidden West* firmly follows our expectations of an attempt to establish order on a chaotic world with unpredictable challenges. Authority is represented by the out-of-control self-replicating robots, and Aloy's quest involves a power struggle to find meaning in the game. There are, however, some more subtle aspects to the game's exploration of social and cultural dimensions; concerns about exponential growth of technology and search for meaning in a world that seems to resist its imposition.

Neale's ideas about the values of hybridisation to the industry in creating successful products apply here. There is clear repetition of many other games in the action-adventure corpus, but also variations, which are mainly those introduced by the hybridised features. The game is often seen as Sony's attempt to create its own version of Nintendo's long-running *Zelda* series. Such a tactic can be risky, but has clearly paid off given *Horizon*'s excellent sales.

The game comfortably demonstrates the generic regime of verisimilitude, primarily through its post-apocalyptic adventure iconography, visual aesthetic and gameplay mechanics. The cultural regime addresses real-world concerns about the environment and the rise of AI and robotics, as well as issues relating to gender and gender politics.

Representations

■ Stuart Hall and the construction of a fantasy world

The *Horizon* series presents us with a post-apocalyptic vision of the future that draws on present-day concerns about the environment and the rise of AI. Social inequality is also shown between rich corporations, represented by the Zenith who fled the original disaster, and the ordinary people, the surviving tribes left behind. As noted in the study of mise en scène, the version of reality encoded in the text is hyperreal in keeping with the symbolic processes and practices of computer games. These include the appearance of characters and game environments that deploy hyperreal colour codes and vivid attention to detail in the dress and non-verbal codes of the characters.

The overall environment of *Horizon* is represented as a map, which can be seen as a version of reality. Given our familiarity with GPS maps that show a satellite view, this adds cultural verisimilitude to the game as it bears some resemblance to a real-world map of present-day western USA – San Francisco features, as do parts of Nevada and Utah. The game includes real-world reference points, such as the ruins of the Golden Gate Bridge and Las Vegas, constructing a post-apocalyptic version of reality where landscapes are familiar but show the passage of time, and landmarks and city spaces have been overgrown and decimated by the events preceding the game series.

■ Feminist theories and gender performativity

As Aloy is a clone of roboticist and generic engineer Dr Elizabeth Sobet, she could be seen as an example of distortion in the roles of women. It is notable that sexist and homophobic reactions from some male game-players online have manifested as:

- dislike of the character's physical appearance, including describing the small hairs on her face as a 'beard'
- creation of memes that denigrate the character's appearance
- disgust that the character is given the opportunity to begin a relationship with another woman in the expansion pack.

These types of reaction can be seen to demonstrate just how much male players are accustomed to the formulation of design and non-verbal codes of female sprites to be pleasing to the male gaze.

We can use the following feminist theories as lenses to view the gender performativity of the role of Aloy.

> **Quick questions**
> 1 Which arbitrary sign features multiple times in the cover art?
> 2 Which stage of Todorov's theory occupies most gameplay hours?
> 3 Explain one feature of game genres that makes them distinct from genres in other media forms.

> **Apply it**
> Visit this fan site, which offers comparisons of locations in the game with their real-world equivalents: horizon.fandom.com/wiki/List_of_Real_Locations_in_Horizon_Forbidden_West.
>
> Explore how the game's graphics construct a post-apocalyptic version of reality.
>
> ■ Which locations bear the strongest resemblance to the present-day world?
> ■ Which are the furthest removed from material reality?

Apply it

Read the following article, which discusses Said's concept of Orientalism in relation to the game and critiques it from this angle: polygon.com/23002044/horizon-forbidden-west-tremortusk-orientalist-tropes.

Make a list of signs or narrative elements that lead the writer to conclude that the game repeats colonialist and Orientalist tropes about people and places.

Quick questions

- Where is the game set, and how does this contribute to its construction of a 'version of reality'?
- Describe one aspect of the game that could be considered problematic when applying a postcolonial reading.
- Which aspect of Aloy's character development caused controversy with male game-players in the expansion?

▽ **Possible applications of feminist ideas to analysis of *Horizon Forbidden West***

Van Zoonen	Aloy is an example of distortion in her representation as a powerful and respected lone female in her version of reality. She moves through the realm able to challenge men and women on equal terms and is fully able to defend herself. Her long hair and braids are conventionally feminine.
bell hooks	Aloy's role as 'white saviour' of the tribes, 'descended' as a clone from an educated white woman, gives her a certain amount of privilege over the women of the tribes. Her braids could be read as signifying cultural appropriation. She moves through the world without facing barriers of intersectionality of class or race.
Judith Butler	Aloy can be seen as a progressive character who is not purely designed for the male gaze and performs an action-based role more commonly associated with masculinity. The revelation of the chapter as gender-queer in the expansion pack, 'Burning Shores', can be seen as transformative and resisting boundaries.

■ Ethnicity and postcolonialism

Within the game, there are tropes that allow us to form a postcolonial reading. For example, the game's narrative uses cultural associations of conquering a frontier, which can be seen as inherently colonial. The various tribes that Aloy must work with are presented as 'other' and language such as 'savage' or 'uncivilised' is used, which has connotations of the legacy of Western colonialist values.

Aloy herself is white and therefore can be interpreted to be positioned as a colonist whose ethical purpose is not open to question or nuance in the mode of address. Her outfit includes tribal attire as well as more sophisticated armour, borrowing from the dress codes of Native American people of frontier times. This could be interpreted as a form of cultural violence, since the colonization of land that belonged to these tribes involved many atrocities.

Aloy's companion from the previous game, Varl, who is black, has an important role in the first part of *Forbidden West*, but is killed off during a quest gameplay and could be read critically as a 'noble savage' whose narrative function is to support the white protagonist.

Audiences

In studying the audiences for *Horizon Forbidden West*, we explore not only the main audience theories as they relate to the product but also how audiences respond to representations within their gameplay and in some cases form a stronger attachment to the text and participate in fan cultures.

■ Psychographics and demographics

For the 16–34 age group, consoles lead the way as the preferred platform for gaming, meaning the potential reach for console games in this sector is impressive (Ofcom, *Online Nation Report 2022*).

Psychographics, or lifestyle profiling, is another method that can be used to explore who the game might appeal to. For example, marketers of console games are keen to appeal to mainstreamers. Mainstreamers buy popular games that have good critical reception and which their friends and acquaintances also play. They prefer big releases over niche games from smaller studios, associating these games with quality of gameplay and increased spectacle, for example in graphics generation.

Female protagonist, female audience?

In the year of *Horizon Forbidden West*'s release, Sony's own data showed that 41 per cent of PS4 and PS5 owners were female. This means that the market must be more responsive than ever to a growing community of dedicated female gamers. Following the introduction of Lara Croft in the *Tomb Raider* series, having a lead female protagonist in an action role has become an accepted part of gaming. Unlike some incarnations of Lara Croft, the character of Aloy is not strongly sexualised, making her less of an object of the male gaze and adding to audience pleasure for women.

Audiences for games – active or passive?

Audience study for computer games must take into account some of the qualities of the mode in which they are consumed, which could affect responses to them. Some of these are:

- Games are potentially more immersive for audiences due to the kinaesthetic nature of gameplay.
- Players may experience the medium differently due to a greater degree of control over the narrative.
- Games can feel more participatory, and practices such as 'modding' (where players rewrite/modify code) can give rise to new, player-created meanings not necessarily sanctioned by the games' creators.
- The amount of hours spent consuming an individual product, and the ability to do this repeatedly as progress is attempted through the game, is significantly different from traditional media.

For these reasons, gaming in general has caused moral panics, with specific games sometimes making headlines due to concerns about content such as the level of violence. These arguments often centre around public opinions about the active or passive nature of computer game consumption as well as concerns about desensitisation to violence and misogyny.

Effects theories

George Gerbner's work on cultivation effects and the mass media suggested that it was the amount of consumption in the long-term that contributed to the shaping of world views and other effects on a person's outlook. For this reason, computer games in general make for an interesting case study, since the hours spent consuming an individual product can be quite high. Gerbner's original study tended to focus on the negative or neutral effects of media consumption, but his model could also offer some different perspectives – for example, we could consider the potential benefits to the self-esteem of young women of immersing themselves in a world like *Horizon Forbidden West* and controlling the actions of a powerful heroine.

The positive and unsexualised representation of Aloy as a female character also offers a different gaming experience for a male audience that may encounter some very different representations of women in other game franchises, promoting equality among game-players and potentially helping shape more positive attitudes to women.

Social learning theory as proposed by Bandura could find issues with the violence in the game – the idea that inflicting violence first hand and seeing gore or injury as entertainment could lead to the acceptability of these acts in the real world. It can be counter-argued, however, that the vast majority of game-players are law-abiding citizens quite able to separate their experience of gameplay from real-world interactions and the fantastical post-apocalyptic landscape from the realm of the real.

■ Reception theory

We can identify different potential responses to the game, but it is on the level of the negotiated reading that player responses may differ most, since there are so many factors, such as mode of gameplay, narrative, graphics and world creation, for players to become familiar with and relate to experience of other games.

The hegemonic reading of the game suggests that the player can fully immerse themselves in the world of the game. In this case, they may already be a fan of the first instalment in the series and therefore be favourably positioned in their expectations of the second.

An oppositional reading would probably lead to a lack of engagement with the game. Perhaps the player would find one of the criticisms levelled at the game too prominent in their own experience. For example:

- seeing the narrative as too complex or nonsensical
- finding the game controls for certain actions (such as climbing) too complex for satisfying gameplay
- being unable to suspend disbelief for other reasons, such as lack of interest in the genre.

■ Fandoms

In an article for *GQ* in 2020, Benjamin McCaw, Narrative Director from Guerilla Games, reported that some players who were given a sneak peak of Aloy were very moved and approached him in tears, visibly affected by the experience of feeling close to the character (gq-magazine.co.uk/culture/article/horizon-forbidden-west-interview).

This demonstrates an acknowledgment on the part of the industry that fans can have an important role in informing the future of a games series. By consulting with players who love the game world and its characters, developers can receive direct feedback on future developments.

According to Henry Jenkins, fans engage with popular culture as interpretative online communities who share their likes and dislikes in a participatory way as a strong part of their identity. These fans demonstrate a strong and more intense engagement with the text beyond that of a typical audience member. Their intense engagement means that they are well positioned to inform the development of the game, as vocal fan likes and dislikes can be translated to the wider audience. Fans can form their own critical communities, with some posts on forums quickly attracting large numbers of responses.

In these, fans compete and collude to demonstrate their own shadow cultural capital and knowledge of the game, as well as participating in expressions of fandom ranging from fan lit and art connected with the game to generating memes and cosplay.

> **Apply it**
>
> Research some examples of fan-forum discussion of the game.
>
> To what extent do individual contributions on discussion threads provide evidence of a hegemonic, negotiated, or oppositional reading? Use quotes from the messages to support your point of view.

▲ An actor cosplays as Aloy at the game premiere in Times Square in New York, 2022

■ The end of the audience

Digital natives, who have grown up with a range of relatively affordable gaming technologies at their disposal, are the biggest consumers of computer games. For this generation, gaming is as much a part of popular culture as television was for previous generations.

Games feed a subculture of online media consumption that is more participatory, from walkthrough videos and release vlogs to fan forums and art. Gaming is a medium that demonstrates very effectively the 'mutuality' of the text and the reader in this multiplicity of additional online activity surrounding consumption. The nature of gameplay means that boundaries between text and context may be increasingly blurred.

Like other digital media products, video games continue to present us with key questions about representational agendas, as we see in discussion of Aloy as a female character. The polarisation of online debates in forums about the game is the best place to see evidence of this.

> **Quick questions**
> 1. Name one quality of computer games as texts that makes them more complex to study using audience theory.
> 2. Describe a hegemonic reading of *Horizon Forbidden West* and the precondition that would make this more likely.
> 3. Explain why a cultivation effect could potentially be positive in the case of this game.

Industries

■ Guerrilla Games – production, distribution and circulation

The studio responsible for the *Horizon* series, Guerilla Games, illustrates some of the structural dimensions to the contemporary gaming industry in terms of production, distribution and circulation. Based in Amsterdam, Guerilla Games is currently owned and controlled by PlayStation Studios, which in turn is a subsidiary of Sony Interactive Entertainment.

Today, many smaller studios and independents increasingly merge and are ultimately purchased by bigger corporations. This often means that they gain exclusive platform rights over the games they produce while retaining the talent that made those studios a success in their earlier independent days.

The table below gives some key moments in Guerilla Games' history.

▼ **Guerilla Games timeline**

2000	Company founded as Lost Boys Games as three Dutch companies merge, before being bought by multimedia company Lost Boys. Initially employed 25 people following merger – quicky expanded to 40.
2001	Merged with Swedish company Icon Medialab and separated off as independent game company.
2003	Acquired by Media Republic (new parent company owned by the previous owner of Lost Boys) and renamed Guerilla Games.
2004	Agreed with Sony Computer Entertainment to exclusively develop content for PlayStation consoles.
2005	Sony Computer Entertainment buys out the studio, which now employs 250 people and plans to expand to 400.
2015	Guerilla Games announces the development of *Horizon Zero Dawn*.
2017	*Horizon Zero Dawn* and an expansion pack for it released on PlayStation 4.
2018	Over 10 million copies of *Horizon* sold, confirming its status as a bestselling game on PS4.
2020	*Horizon Forbidden West* announced in development.
2022	*Horizon Forbidden West* released (with an expansion pack in 2023) for PS5.
2023	New game is announced in collaboration with British studio Firesprite (acquired by Sony in 2021) for PS5 and PSVR2.

Structuring of media industry around gaming platforms

There are clear benefits for a media conglomerate to owning both the gaming platform itself and the content it produces. By targeting for buy-outs indie developers who have produced content that sells well across platforms, companies gain exclusive rights to content and the pool of talent that created it. Successful games become associated with the corporate brand and may lead more players to buy into their set-ups. So, games series are also popular with big labels: they encourage brand loyalty and retain the interest of consumers.

For the companies acquired, there may be the possibility of expansion, investment and, in theory, protection from the ups and downs of the market and audience reception to individual products. Companies taking this decision must weigh these benefits against the loss of autonomy and potential stifling of creative projects that may not fit with the parent company's market profile.

Regulation

In the UK, games are regulated by the Games Rating Authority, which is part of the Video Standards Council. The GRA uses the PEGI game rating system, which is widely recognised by game-players and trusted by parents of younger players.

Horizon Forbidden West is rated PEGI 16, meaning that depictions of violence or sexual activity can appear realistic, and bad language and drug, alcohol and tobacco use may all be depicted.

The Games Rating Authority (GRA) website shows the assessment of the gameplay in relation to key issues for regulators: gamesratingauthority.org.uk/RatingBoard/games/?q=horizon.

The website also provides information aimed at parents about game content and age ratings: gamesratingauthority.org.uk/RatingBoard.

Apply it

Using the GRA rating details and your previous viewing of game walkthroughs, discuss the following issues relating to game regulation with specific reference to *Horizon Forbidden West*.

- Does it make a difference to audience reception whether violence is enacted in a fantasy context or a representation of the 'real' world?
- Why might issues such as bad language or violence be of concern to media regulators with games – are there any differences between the way in which games are consumed and other media products?

For more on games regulation in the UK, see Chapter 7 of the Student Book.

Lunt and Livingstone's work on media regulation tells us that the role of a regulator must balance the need to protect citizens from potentially harmful or disturbing content while allowing consumers the right to consume a range of media products and make their own decisions about suitability. This means trying to protect both children and vulnerable people while still allowing them to participate in an enjoyable pastime that is deeply embedded in pop culture.

In their paper 'The regulator, the public and the media', Lunt and Livingstone assert that the public often hold paradoxical views of regulation versus risk, in that people are strongly in favour of personal choice and responsibility in terms of consuming media, but, at the same time, they want support in understanding what can be quite complex details about the project, and have concerns that some people are more vulnerable and should be protected from harmful influences (eprints.lse.ac.uk/24556/1/The_regulator_the_public_and_the_media_%28LSERO%29.pdf).

Under UK law, all games sold must receive a rating, and outlets that supply them are expected to comply with age restrictions and ask for evidence of age if they suspect a customer is younger than the game rating. However, an adult may legally gift a game of any age rating to a child – at this point it is up to the parent to make an individual judgement about suitability for their individual child. It could be argued that this is a difficult decision for parents to make since:

- the immersive properties of games mean children spend many hours playing them, meaning their level of repeated exposure to unsuitable content is higher than, for example, watching a film
- parents may not be aware of issues relating to media desensitisation and child development
- parents may not monitor fully what children are playing – if they are not gamers themselves, they may not know what the content is like
- the rating categories are necessarily broad – a child may cope well with violence in one game but not another
- individual maturity of children as they grow up varies between siblings, and many families will find younger players exposed to games their older siblings play and therefore want to play them
- 'vulnerable people' are difficult to define – a mental illness might make someone more susceptible to media effects, for example – but it would be difficult to argue that anyone with a mental illness should be barred from playing certain games based on an age certificate.

Quick questions
1. Which British studio's development services have been acquired by Sony in the increasing expansion of its *Horizon* series development?
2. Which website in the UK can be visited to find age ratings and content advice for all games that are legally available in the region?

Further reading

- 'The regulator, the public and the media: Imagining a role for the public in communication regulation', paper by key thinkers Lunt and Livingstone discussing the delicate balance faced by regulators of media content in a UK context: eprints.lse.ac.uk/24556/1/The_regulator_the_public_and_the_media_%28LSERO%29.pdf.
- *UK Games Industry Census 2022*, interesting analysis of diversity in the gaming industry: ukie.org.uk/resources/uk-games-industry-census-2022.
- Lively game review in *The Guardian*: theguardian.com/games/2022/feb/14/horizon-forbidden-west-review-an-eccentric-adventure-with-robot-dinosaurs
- 'Data lost, forbidden or controlled? The Archivists of *Horizon Forbidden West*' by Ashley Lanni, academic paper on the cultural and social meanings of information and data collection in the game: ideaexchange.uakron.edu/docam/vol10/iss1/7.
- '*Horizon Zero Dawn* and *Horizon Forbidden West*', scholarly article on the game as an example of a post-apocalyptic narrative: cdamm.org/articles/horizon-zero-dawn-and-horizon-forbidden-west.

Photo credits

Photos reproduced by permission of: **p.2** *l* © Walik Goshorn/Mediapunch/Alamy Stock Photo, *bl* © Jordan Strauss/Invision/AP/Alamy Stock Photo; **p.4** *tl* © Everett Collection, Inc./Alamy Stock Photo, *bl* © Paramount Pictures/Photo 12/Alamy Stock Photo; **p.5** © 20TH CENTURY FOX/Album/Alamy Stock Photo; **p.6** *b* © Pictorial Press Ltd/Alamy Stock Photo, *bl* © Bill Waterson/Alamy Stock Photo; **p.7** *tr* © RiskyWalls/Alamy Stock Photo, *c* © John Carucci/Associated Press/Alamy Stock Photo; **p.8** © TY Lim/Shutterstock.com; **p.10** © GRANGER - Historical Picture Archive/Alamy Stock Photo; **p.13** © Chris Pizzello/Associated Press/Alamy Stock Photo; **p.16** © Roberto Herrett/Alamy Stock Photo; **p.18** Copyright Guardian News & Media Ltd 2024; **p.20** Copyright Guardian News & Media Ltd 2024; **p.25** © Landmark Media/Alamy Stock Photo; **p.26** *c* © Ron Harvey/New Line Cinema/Courtesy Everett Collection/Alamy Stock Photo, *l* © Ron Harvey/New Line Cinema/Courtesy Everett Collection/Alamy Stock Photo; **p.28** © Lifestyle pictures/Alamy Stock Photo; **p.34** BBC/James Mobbs; **p.37** © Phil Stafford/Shutterstock.com; **p.38** © Featureflash Photo Agency/Shutterstock.com; **p.39** © Featureflash Photo Agency/Shutterstock.com; **p.42** © Elizabeth Goodenough/Everett Collection/Alamy Stock Photo; **p.47** © Danmarks Radio/TCD/Prod.DB/Alamy Stock Photo; **p.51** © Chris Radburn/PA Images/Alamy Stock Photo; **p.53** *l* © Gai/TCD/Prod.DB/Alamy Stock Photo, *r* © Trinity Mirror/Mirrorpix/Alamy Stock Photo; **p.54** *l* © LONDON FILMS/Album/Alamy Stock Photo, *r* © Kpa Publicity Stills/United Archives GmbH/Alamy Stock Photo; **p.55** © Photo12/7e Art/Tine Harden/Danmarks Radio/Alamy Stock Photo; **p.57** © Archives du 7e Art/Photo 12/Alamy Stock Photo; **p.60** *t* © Myles Aronowitz/Netflix/Courtesy Everett Collection/Alamy Stock Photo, *c* © Collection Christophel/ITV/DR Photo Patrick REDMOND/Alamy Stock Photo; **p.61** *tl* © GAUMONT TELEVISION/Album/Alamy Stock Photo, *bl* © Emmanuel Guimier/Netflix/The Hollywood Archive/American Pictorial Collection/PictureLux/Alamy Stock Photo; **p.62** *tr* © Emmanuel Guimier/Netflix/The Hollywood Archive/American Pictorial Collection/PictureLux/Alamy Stock Photo, *r* © Emmanuel Guimier/Netflix/The Hollywood Archive/American Pictorial Collection/PictureLux/Alamy Stock Photo; **p.77** © Homer Sykes/Alamy Stock Photo; **p.78** © Pictorial Press Ltd/Alamy Stock Photo; **p.80** © RW/MediaPunch/Alamy Stock Photo; **p.89** © RW/MediaPunch/Alamy Stock Photo.